❖

The Inner Stage

❖

The Inner Stage

*Finding a Center
in Prayer and Ritual*

James Roose~Evans

COWLEY PUBLICATIONS
Cambridge, Massachusetts

Published in Great Britain in 1987 by Rider &
Company, an imprint of Century Hutchinson Ltd,
under the title, *Inner Journey, Outer Journey*

Published in the United States of America by Cowley
Publications, a division of the Society of St. John the
Evangelist.

ISBN: 1-56101-001-4
Library of Congress Number: 89-29269

Cover illustration and design by Daniel Earl Thaxton

Library of Congress Cataloging-in-Publication Data
Roose-Evans, James.
    [Inner Journey, outer journey]
    The inner stage / James Roose-Evans.
        p. cm.
    Reprint. Originally published: Inner journey, outer
journey. London: Rider, 1987.
        ISBN: 1-56101-001-4 : $9.95
        1. Spiritual life—Anglican authors. 2. Roose-Evans,
James.
    I. Title.
    [BV4501.2.R6655 1987]
    245.4'83—dc20   89-29269
                                           CIP

This book is printed on acid-free paper and was
produced in the United States of America.

Cowley Publications
980 Memorial Drive
Cambridge, Massachusetts 02138

This book is dedicated in loving memory
of my first teacher
Franz Elkisch, MD
to
Meinrad Craighead
who, as a member of the community at Stanbrook Abbey
gave so richly of her friendship and prayer
and
The Rt. Rev. Jerome Hodkinson, OSB,
whose friendship and prayers have sustained me
over thirty years,
while it was in the chapel of St Benedict at Belmont Abbey that
there came the command, 'Write your book.'

Cowley Publications

is a ministry of the Society of St. John the Evangelist, a religious community for men in the Episcopal Church. Emerging from the Society's tradition of prayer, theological reflection and diversity of mission, Cowley Publications is centered in the rich heritage of the Anglican Communion.

Cowley Publications seeks to provide books, audio cassettes, and other resources for the ongoing theological exploration and spiritual development of the Episcopal Church and other churches in the body of Christ. To this end, Cowley Publications is dedicated to developing a new generation of theological writers, encouraging them to produce timely, creative and stimulating publications of excellence, and making these publications available widely, reaching both clergy and lay persons.

❖

Table of Contents

❖

Acknowledgements

I would like to thank my close friend John Hencher, priest of the Hereford diocese, who was the signpost that pointed me towards ordination; the Rt Rev. John Easthaugh, Bishop of Hereford, who understood and sent me to Glasshampton Monastery; Brother Alban of the Society of St Francis who was then Guardian of the monastery; Brother David, with whom I spent long hours in the chapel; Hywel Jones, whose wisdom, love and humour have nourished me; Rev. David Shapland and Canon Laurence Reading, who probed and tested; and Canon Murray Irvine, my Director of Ordinands; and the Rt Rev. Kenneth Woolcombe, the Rev. Prebendary Ernest Chitty, and Rev. Graham Dowell who, especially during one bewildering year, strongly supported me. I would also like to thank my friend, Cynthia Charlesworth, whose prayers have so often lightened the burden; James Malcolm, chairman of the Theater Department at Colorado College, Colorado Springs, who, by inviting me to teach a course on ritual in the spring of 1985, enabled me to start writing this book; John Lahr, who championed my earlier book, *Experimental Theatre,* and so opened a door to Colorado; Oliver Caldecott, my editor at Century-Hutchinson, whose perception has added so immeasurably to this book.

James Roose-Evans

Prologue

In the early 1960s, shortly after founding the Hampstead Theatre, I was asked as a layman to do a series of *Epilogues* for television on the subject of prayer. Previous to this I had been host of a weekly programme for teenagers presented by the Churches, entitled *Sunday Break*. Then, in 1970, over a period of several months I wrote a short weekly column for *The Church Times* on meditation. The response revealed that there were many Christians trying to learn a form of meditation suitable to their needs and religious perspective. Slowly, over the years, in the midst of a full and active life in theatre, as artistic director of the Hampstead Theatre, then freelance director and writer, this book has grown. On St David's Day 1981 I was given the diaconate at Glasshampton Monastery in Worcestershire by the Bishop of Hereford, the Rt Rev. John Easthaugh. Four months later I was ordained a non-stipendiary priest in Hereford Cathedral. I continue to work in the theatre, write books, lead workshops and serve when needed in a public capacity as priest, be this in Herefordshire, London, New York or Colorado – wherever, in fact, my work takes me.

This book is in three sections. The first, The Traveller, offers a glimpse of the traveller himself, but no more than a glimpse for this is not intended to be an autobiography. The middle section, The Map, is an account of the practice of wordless prayer to which I was led. It describes a *bhakti* form of prayer. There are many ways of praying, but I can only speak of what I know. *Bhakti* means prayer of the heart, the simple response of the inner self to the Divine Self. The third and final section, The Journeying, represents a series of reflections while journeying with the map, one for each day of the month. Prayer can only be crept up on slowly, and so it seemed good to balance the concentrated instruction of the middle section with a more leisurely conversation.

It is a book aimed at those Christians who have moved beyond a rote Christianity which basically emphasizes 'morality' issues, and who feel drawn to contemplative prayer and/or meditation as a way of finding a spiritual centre to their lives, and are looking for guidance; for the many Christians who are taught virtually nothing about contemplative prayer in the Church today and who are struggling, intuitively, very much on their own as I was, to find a deeper level of prayer. Finally, it is for those seekers after truth who find it difficult to relate to existing forms of Christianity. Many people today, while sympathetic to the Church and the ancient truths that it teaches and represents, nevertheless find that many of these truths are being taught more effectively outside the institutional churches. There is a gap widening between religion and spirituality and there is an urgent need for bridges to be built. It is to provide one such bridge that this book has been written.

ACT ONE: The Traveller

Make me to see and hear that I may know
This journey and the place towards which I go;
For a beginning and an end are mine
Surely, and have their sign
Which I and all in the earth and heavens show.
Teach me to know.

If I could truly know that I do know
This, and the foreshower of this show,
Who is myself, for plot and scene are mine,
They say, and the world my sign,
Man, earth, and heaven, co-patterned so and so —
If I could know.

Edwin Muir
Collected Poems

1

Finding the Centre

If I pass an enclosed garden with a gate or door in the wall, I love to open it and peer inside. If there is no gate I may jump up and, clinging to the wall, look over into the garden on the other side. I am not envious of other people's gardens, but I like to know that they are there. Under the Gardens of England scheme many individuals open up their gardens for a few days each year in order to share them with the public, while the National Trust often opens its gardens for the whole year.

We may not have a garden and may have no intention of starting one, not even a window box; yet we are enriched by the experience of walking in other people's gardens. We are enriched just by knowing that they are there as different ways of living. So it is with this book which, in a much smaller form, was originally printed privately and anonymously and shared with a few people. Now it is being opened to the public in general. Much of it is written in a practical way because prayer, like gardening, is a very practical business. I do not assume that every reader is going to start praying, any more than the average visitor to a National Trust garden is intending to start a garden. However, among the thousands who visit those gardens you will often come across someone peering at a plant and its metal tag, scribbling the name on the back of an envelope, even buying a specimen from the garden shop. That person will return home bearing a memory of that visit, which is then firmly planted in his or her own soil. Sometimes, even, rounding the corner of a yew hedge at Powis Castle, I have often surprised some genteel lady discreetly taking a cutting with a pair of nail scissors, popping it into some rooting powder – conveniently kept in a pill box – then placing it inside a plastic bag and dropping that into her handbag. In one way or another these cuttings, like ideas, will reappear years hence as bushes, plants or trees in other gardens. Hopefully, in the same way, this book may provide the reader who already meditates or prays with fresh cuttings; or it may encourage someone to start their own interior garden.

There will be those who, reading this, will ask how a man of the theatre comes to be writing a book on meditation or contemplative prayer. After all, theatre is one of the toughest and most egocentric of professions. Recently, in an interview from Hollywood, the actress Helen Mirren remarked, 'As an actress you've got to look at "I", to learn to be unafraid of your own horrible ego. Americans are totally about "I".' Theatre people are not exactly humble and they do tend to enjoy the limelight a good deal. In the media they often receive what to many must seem an inordinate amount of attention. Then, too, the life of someone in show business can appear to the outsider as highly exotic, full of variety and surprise, unlike the duller, more predictable life patterns of most people. What the public does not see, of course, are the long periods of unemployment when no work comes or, if it does, is unsuitable. It is a profession full of insecurities and uncertainties, without logic. Most people who do a job well expect continuing promotion, but in show business it is not like that at all. Actors, directors and designers, writers too, rise and fall with alarming rapidity, often for no discernible reason; a highly esteemed actor, with a family to support, can find himself on the poverty line – even below it – while a less able actor who happens to have a good year with a few commercials can earn more than the Prime Minister. In England and the USA the majority are unemployed for the greater part of each year. A writer can always write, and a painter can always paint, but actors, dancers, directors and designers can only work if someone employs them.

For those of us who work in show business it is an itinerant and uncertain life, and in order to survive we have to find a centre within our self. That centre, quite obviously, cannot be solely our work. Of course, this is increasingly true of everyone. Today it is no longer enough to say: I am an actor, a miner, a builder, a farm labourer, a nurse. As automation takes over so many jobs, the changing pattern of our society is forcing us all to find an identity that lies deeper, and to realize that work is not necessarily equated with our job. Even in family situations, as rôles are reversed, where Dad becomes Mum, and Mum goes out to work, the issues of identity are becoming increasingly complex. Yet if we can measure up to the challenge there is an unique opportunity here for growth, both in ourselves as individuals and as a society. The changing social and economic patterns are forcing us to find new answers to the questions: Who am I? Where have I come from? Where am I going?

When I was auditioning actors for my adaptation of Laurie Lee's *Cider with Rosie* I received over five hundred letters from actors wanting to be in the production. In the end I selected some three hundred and gave each a fifteen minute audition, a process which took three weeks, and out of that number seven were selected. For the thousands waiting for a chance to act, only a few make it. As Cassie sings in the musical *A Chorus Line*, 'I am a dancer. Let me dance for you. Let me try or I die!' Watching that film it struck me forcibly that showbiz is very much a metaphor for life itself, and there is one scene in the show which illustrates this. Cassie, who is a solo dancer of quality but has been out of work for two years, insists on being auditioned for the chorus line of the brilliant but ruthless choreographer's new show. He can't believe that she is serious.

'Is that what you really want?' he asks. 'To be in the chorus line?'

She replies, 'That's where I belong.'

'But you're *special*!' he retorts, at which she cries out passionately, pointing to the other dancers on the stage, '*Everyone* up there is special!'

Unless we believe that each one of us is special, then life indeed is no more than a series of meaningless auditions for a remote and uncaring director. Unless we can find meaning and significance in our lives we shall be trapped in a ceaseless round of meaningless activity. Each one of us has to find a centre within.

The way to that centre is hard. All legends and fairy stories that speak of the heroine or hero setting forth on a quest tell the same tale. Many people never even set out on their own individual quest or, if they do, become quickly trapped by their anger, prejudice and personal blocks. It is not surprising that in the 1960s and 1970s many people were drawn into encounter and similar therapy groups, aware of a hunger for something that they could not find in their religion, school, college – even their own family. This was especially true in America, where there was, and still is, a hunger for relationships which can be real and close, in which feelings and emotions are spontaneously expressed without first being carefully censored or bottled up; where deep experiences, whether of joy or grief, are capable of being shared; where an individual can be both known and accepted, and know that further growth is possible. However, in the 1980s has come an awareness that, valuable and enriching as such encounters can be, there is yet more – the realization as an American psychiatrist has recently observed, that the basic urge of the human being is to worship. 'This urge is deeper than the sex urge. It is experienced from the infant stage to the very aged. The human must look to something greater than he is, something in which he can feel secure because he believes it to be right, changeless, wise, powerful, eternal.' He must have such a power to trust or he does not have the urge to progress. To cut off this need to worship is like cutting off the main root of a tree.

I am convinced that many more people feel this need to worship than is perhaps admitted or even comprehended, but they do not know what to do with it. The form of public worship that is to be found in many churches, chapels, synagogues and temples alienates them. Some respond to such ceremonies and ritual, finding in them the roots of their own buried tradition; but many can find no way of relating to them, and so are left with this desire to worship and nowhere to go. As a senior cardinal at the Synod of Bishops in Rome in November 1985 observed, 'People are searching for the sacred in their lives – but outside the Church.' As a culture we are ritually out of phase. We are, if at all, dragooned into rituals (even fraternity rituals) that mean little or nothing to us, yet when we need the symbolic deepening of an important experience we somehow lack the necessary gestures and images. No wonder, says Harvey Cox, the American theologian, that we undergo identity crises until we die.

Worship begins, however, as an interior activity, and that is where each of us can start. Another name for this is prayer. If worship means to adore or venerate that which is divine, to show respect and devotion to that which is above and beyond us, then prayer is any form of spiritual communion with that deity. Each one of us has to set out on this journey alone. It is only as we journey that we meet others also travelling this path, and so we discover gradually that we are part of a whole worshipping community, not bound by or within the walls of any one sect or tradition but, rather, experiencing the fact that the whole earth worships. We may, on the way, build temples and holy places, but each of us begins with the temple that is within.

The little that I know about prayer – and it is indeed very little – has been forged in the fire of practice, against a backdrop of uncertainty, stress and lack of security, in a restless, hustling profession. I am not an authority on prayer; if indeed such a thing is possible, for prayer can never be won. It is too like the game of Snakes and Ladders: no sooner do we reach the top of the ladder than we fall back several places. All that any of us can do is to share with one another our experience, in the way that gardeners do, and encourage one another. To that extent it may be an encouragement to others to know that in such a gipsy existence as mine has been, hanging onto the cliff face of what at times has often seemed an unending climb, with rope and nerves and energies wearing thin, an inner centre can be found and held. Rather, as a friend once remarked about Assisi, 'Ultimately it is a place inside you. It is there, wherever you go.' So it is with the life of prayer. When we have gained this interior silence we can carry it around with us in the world and pray everywhere. This interior silence can grow, provided we tend it as regularly as a hothouse plant. As the Curé d'Ars* once said, 'My children, your hearts are small, but prayer enlarges them and renders them capable of loving God.'

When I was at Oxford the only books on silent prayer that I could find were powerful works by great saints or by professional religious. The great authority with which they spoke made them

*St John Mary Vianney, more popularly know as the Curé d'Ars. Born in Lyons, France, in 1786, he was parish priest of Ars until his death in 1859. His help to those who came to him in the confessional was renowned and people flocked from all sides to obtain his advice. His feast is celebrated on August 4th.

all seem very daunting. In the past two decades, however, many books have been written by people who are neither priests nor religious – books by ordinary people who have learned how to meditate and pray. As more people learn, so the variety of approaches increases; as a result prayer becomes not something remote for the so-called specialist, but a homely and natural activity. Once we have found our way into this deep inner life of prayer, that form of prayer which is without words, and which is described in the section entitled *The Map*, it becomes like a seed planted within us – we have only to water it regularly, and it will send down deep roots and grow into our own tree.

Most people's lives follow the same fundamental pattern – the first half is centred upon the ego, upon the thrust of achievement and ambition, and the second half upon the discovery of the Self or god within. The first journey is outer and the second inner. For myself it has been somewhat different – I cannot speak of an outer and inner journey as two separate journeys. From a very early age I appear to have had an awareness of a deeper pattern to life, and if much of those early games and rituals was play-acting (I recall that, among many things, I made a chapel in the garden) it was, nonetheless, a form of theatre that was ritual, a series of spontaneous and creative expressions of this awareness of another 'order'. That ritual and theatre are closely related is something I have grown to understand and now use as the basis of workshops on ritual which I teach in America – where there is a particular hunger for such things. By this I do not mean 'church' or liturgical ritual, but those original rituals that articulate and enshrine the deepest aspirations of an individual or a group of people at a particular moment of time, and that are created by them. Through the making of such rituals the individual is often enabled to return to a living participation in the rituals of her or his own tradition. In many churches, temples and synagogues the rituals have fossilised, have become genteel or glib from familiar repetition. The spirit has gone out of the original form. Again, it is not so much an alternative liturgy or ritual that is called for as growth and change from within. When people are alive to the richness of symbol in the liturgy of their faith, it will be because they are alive to the richness of symbol everywhere.

Some people today claim that God is solely immanent – that is,

hidden away somewhere in the psyche. But God is also transcendent, outside and beyond the present dimension of time and
space. To be truly *homo religiosus* (a religious person), one must
bring together the outside and the inside, finding God both 'out
there' and 'in here'. It is here that the creative process comes into
its own, assisting the spiritual process. From childhood onwards
my ability at certain moments, to act out or visualize, through
dance, gesture, movement, sound, drawing, painting or words,
these inner states of worship, as also of conflict, yearning, lust,
love, anger and jealousy, has enabled me to shed skins and go on
growing. By visualizations and by acting out it is possible to bring
together the outer and the inner in our daily living. The creative
process enables us to absorb experience with our whole being, to
give it a form and shape, thereby enhancing our capacity to live.
As the American poet Robert Frost once said to me, 'Each poem
that I write is one more stay against confusion.' By gaining
conscious control of unconscious imagery we bring into order
our own chaotic psyches. It is a process of self-healing. The songs
and dances, the drawings and carvings, the poems and rituals and
ceremonials that come forth from the depths of our own beings
enable us to master those emotions which might otherwise
overwhelm us, enabling each of us, through histrionic or other
creative means, to understand our own condition more clearly. In
his book *Archetypal Medicine** Dr Alfred Ziegler writes, 'The
most important thing is to see this theatre that we are. A readiness
to integrate all kinds of *shadow*. . . . We never know how much
we may prevent diseases by artistic fantasies that change the
mood, the attitude.' As the American pioneer of ritual, Anna
Halprin, said to me recently in California, 'Art is an enduring
process for it touches on the spiritual dimension in a way that no
other human activity does. In art you are able to give expression
to that which lies deep inside you and, having given expression to
it, you receive back a vision which is a map by which you can set
your other goals.' Thirty years ago Anna Halprin founded one of
the most dynamic performing groups in America, the Dancers'
Workshop. Like others of her contemporaries in theatre,
however, she began to question the rôle of the audience today.

*(Spring Publications, Dallas, 1985)

She no longer felt it sufficient for a professional group to be creating art for a passive audience and so she began to work with non-professionals, groups of ordinary people of all ages, cultures and backgrounds, helping them to create their own rituals. In this she was very much ahead of her time. It is only now, faced with greater automation, as people move into a shorter working week and a shorter working life, that the question of what they will do with their greatly increased leisure time becomes one of the most urgent sociological, psychological and spiritual problems of our time. What people like Anna Halprin are discovering is that the majority of people possess, no matter how unused, real creative and imaginative faculties.

We need to rediscover how to give form to our most urgent feelings, aspirations and fears, so that we may understand ourselves better through movement, colour, rhythm, music, ritual and ceremonial; in our creation of a home, of a garden, of a relationship; in our living, in our loving, and in our dying; as well as in a work of craft or art. We have to learn how to respond directly and truly to our deepest impulses and to give them form and rhythm; like the youth Tito who, at the close of Herman Hesse's *The Glass Bead Game*, quite unselfconsciously begins to dance on the mountain top as the sun rises. 'Without knowing what he was doing, asking no questions, he obeyed the command of the ecstatic moment, danced his worship, prayed to the sun, professed with devout movements and gestures his joy, his faith in life.'

Those who are fortunate to take part in the workshops of Anna Halprin or Jerzy Grotowski (the Polish theatre director) know what it is to live and move from their own centre. A psychiatrist who took part in one of Grotowski's workshops in Poland observed,

> I would like to meet such people all the time, people who have been awakened, who are wide open to receive reality. People who participate in the drama of life, their own and that of other people. It seems to me that this work turns passive participants, through action, into actors of their fate. It seems to me that this is one of the forms of theatre of the future. What matters is to bring out the vitality inherent in every man, and once it has been brought out, to enrich life itself so that it can become again the source of strength for culture and for the theatre.

Thus we may speak truly of the healing arts, for art at its deepest level has this ability to heal and to make whole; and at the moment when worship enters into our rituals and ceremonials they are transformed into sacred art. This relationship of creativity and spirituality is something that the majority of clergy do not understand. 'The act of poetry,' says the young poet Caitlin Matthews, 'is being aware of one's destiny and of the will of God.' Art, like prayer, is a deep underground river. But so much that passes for religious art, like so much religious practice, is, in the words of the poet and pontiff Karol Wojtyla, 'still far from the source'.

Although I was born in London, I was brought up mainly in the country. I went to some fifteen schools and we lived in many more homes. My mother loved moving and the challenge of creating new homes but it had an unsettling effect, especially on my education. Not until, at the age of fourteen, I went to live with friends who taught me discipline and many other skills, encouraging me to realize that I had a brain, did I rise from bottom of the class to top and succeed in winning a place to New College, Oxford. I was not baptized until I was five years old, and it was on my own initiative later that I found my way to church and got myself confirmed. By the time I was sixteen I was quite clear that one day I would be received into the Roman Catholic Church, although I knew that the time had not yet arrived. In 1945 I was conscripted into the Army to do my eighteen months' National Service and towards the end of that time posted to Trieste. There I learned to speak Italian and was finally received into the Roman Church. The experience of that culture and the natural way Italians have of wandering in and out of church at all times of the day – pausing with armfuls of shopping, and accompanied by small children – to light candles and say a prayer or two, was to me an air that I breathed deeply. It became, and remains, central to my whole life. I was seeing religion not as a Sunday activity, set apart, but impregnating the whole of one's life. Churches ought to be more like Hindu or Buddhist temples, or Muslem mosques – holy places where there is a constant coming and going, every hour of the day, of people dropping in for a chat with God. Recently I mentioned this to a friend, who replied, 'I often take Holly (her grandchild, aged three) to Westminster Cathedral

(London's Roman Catholic Cathedral). It's so alive, with all the candles glittering, and people praying. It has such a sense of being a special place. I'm Anglican, but most Anglican churches are so dead – you couldn't take a child into them. Holly loves it. "We're going to talk to Jesus!" she says.'

After my first communion on 6 June 1948, at the Church of St Vincent de Paul in Trieste, I was standing on the steps outside, surrounded by my Italian godparents and their friends, when I heard the parish priest say to me, '*È contento adesso?*' I learned then for the first time the importance of tone of voice and the limitation of words as signs, at least outside of poetry. All attempts to translate those words are somehow inadequate compared with the emotion in his voice and what I was feeling: *You are content now? You are happy? You have arrived?* I knew only that I had come home.

When I returned to England and left the Army I gave up my place at Oxford, determined to become an actor. I tried twice for the Royal Academy of Dramatic Art and failed; I tried once – a second attempt not permitted – for the old Vic School, and failed. I entered a small dramatic academy run by an elderly actor and his wife, and left after one week. I then enrolled in a theatre studio, the Hovel, run supposedly on Stanislavsky's principles; however I left after one term when its principal, Lady Neysa Graham, attempting to expound Stanislavsky's theories of acting, said, 'Oh, James, you tell them, you understand it better'! Unable to find the training that I sought, going the rounds of agents, doing one-night stands in halls where the audiences sat at tables drinking beer from large enamel jugs and talking and smoking throughout the performance, coupled with a traumatic home situation, it is perhaps not surprising that I had a nervous breakdown. I was sent by my confessor to a Jungian analyst, Dr Franz Elkisch. This analysis was to continue, with breaks, over the next twenty-five years. Franz Elkisch was a German Jew, trained by Jung, who had managed to escape from Germany just before the outbreak of war. He arrived in England penniless and speaking no English. His wife Paula, also an analyst, fled to New York. Franz became a convert to Catholicism and was received into the Church at Downside Abbey by Dom Hubert van Zeller.

The discovery of the inner realms within each one of us is a rich

and dangerous process and we need a guide who will protect us
on such a journey. I was fortunate that I was sent to a Jungian and
doubly fortunate that I was sent to the right person from the start.
The inner world of the unconscious which I then began to
uncover in dreams and paintings is a territory as wonderful and
awesome as that of Perelandra in C.S. Lewis's novel and as
dangerous as the journeys of Odysseus. Indeed, the story of
Odysseus is a mythical telling of all such journeys into these inner
realms. To venture alone into them is both foolhardy and
perilous. The waters of the unconscious can swiftly engulf, and
those who flirt with the unconscious take great risks. Once, in the
South of France, I was invited by the late Eileen Garrett ('the most
unique medium in the Western world', as *The Sunday Times* once
described her) to take LSD in clinical conditions but, in spite of
several years of analysis (or perhaps because of?), I declined. I am
by nature a radical, an explorer, yet in this instance I sensed that
under the influence of LSD I might encounter some of my own
demons and not perhaps be strong enough, psychically or
spiritually, to handle the situation.

All fables, fairy stories and myths indicate the need for a guide
on such a journey. Given the external guide, then a series of
internal guides begin to manifest themselves in dreams and
visualizations. Often it is a wise old woman or man who is one's
teacher, often an animal, but the teacher or guide is capable of
appearing in less familiar guises; and here it is important to
understand Jung's definition of the shadow side of the self, those
aspects of our selves that are unrealized and, for that reason,
feared. This is why the 'teacher within' so often appears in the
form of a faceless person, a shabby, threatening tramp, a highly
erotic figure, or a dangerous animal, as in the story of the Princess
and the Frog, or Beauty and the Beast. For St Francis of Assisi it
was the decaying, diseased leper that had to be embraced; for
Theseus it was the Minotaur, that monster, half-human and
half-animal, which lurks within the labyrinth of each one of us,
that had to be met, tamed and overcome. Hidden within the
uncomfortable, threatening or disturbing figure is the truth we
have yet to learn. It is in the desert that we find the signpost; in a
field of excrement that we discover the pearl of great price; or

when a dark cloud descends and we can no longer see the way
forward that a voice speaks to us:

> A voice I did not know said to me:
> I freed your shoulder from the burden;
> Your hands were freed from the load.
> You called in distress and I saved you.
> I answered, concealed in the storm cloud,
> At the waters of Meribah I tested you.
>
> (Psalm 81.)

A true analysis should lead to *metanoia*, a complete change. It
is a process brought about not by intellectual debate but by direct
experience. The definition of the word 'experience' is itself a key
to this whole process. It means to attempt, venture or risk,
whence the Greek *peira* is the source of our word 'empirical'.
More directly it derives, via Middle English and Old French, from
the Latin *experientia* – denoting trial, proof, experiment – itself
generated from *experiens*, the present participle of *experii* – to
try, to test, from *ex* (out) plus the base *per*, as in *peritus*, meaning
experienced, having learned by trying. The suffixed, extended
form of *per* is *peri-to*, from which comes *periculum*, meaning
trial, danger, peril. Experience is linked with risk, straining
towards drama, crisis, rather than cognitive learning. Thus the
Greek verb, as Victor Turner demonstrates in *From Ritual to
Theatre*, means 'pass through', hence the idea of experience as
perilous passage, even rite of passage. From *per* also we derive
our words 'fare' and 'ferry'. In this way, Turner explains, we have
in the word 'experience' the cumulative ideas of a journey, a test,
a ritual passage, an exposure to peril or risk, and a source of fear.
By means of experience we fare fearfully through perils, taking
experimental steps.

Somewhere about the time that I was trying to carve my first
steps in the theatre, I found myself staying at Ampleforth Abbey
in Yorkshire, where I fell in love with the monastic way of life. I
went to the Abbot and said that I would like to be accepted as a
novice. He, wisely, suggested I should go to Oxford to take a
degree, and I was given a place to read English at St Benet's Hall,
the House of Studies for the Congregation of English Benedictines. This, his explained, would give me a chance to find out

more about what kind of person I was and also what kind of people monks were. A fellow student – we shared the same tutor and sat opposite each other in the refectory – was a monk at Belmont Abbey in Herefordshire, Jerome Hodkinson, subsequently to become Abbot there.

When I went down, having gained an honours degree, I knew that my work lay in the theatre. I became an actor in repertory, graduating to leading man. Through the intervention of Kenneth Williams, the juvenile charactor actor in the company, I was persuaded to direct one of the productions. After that experience I knew that my various talents – writing, acting, directing, designing, the dance – all found their fullest use in the art of directing. Then in 1954 I was given the opportunity of running my first theatre, the Maddermarket Theatre in Norwich, an Elizabethan-style playhouse founded by Nugent Monck, a protégé of William Poel who had revolutionized the staging and speaking of Shakespeare. Already, however, I had met the great American dancer and choreographer, Martha Graham, who was to be a turning point in my life.

In Herman Hesse's novel *Steppenwolf*, the owner of the Magic Theatre says to the hero, 'It is the world of your own soul that you seek. Only within yourself exists that other reality for which you long. I can give you nothing that has not already its own being within yourself. I can throw open to you no picture gallery but your own soul. All I can give you is the opportunity, the impulse, the key. I help you to make your own world visible.' Not until 1954, when I encountered the dance theatre of Martha Graham, did I discover that theatre could be expressive of those interior realms that I had sensed as a child and was now encountering in my analysis. Here was the kind of theatre for which I had been looking. Martha Graham helped to make visible, in the medium of theatre, my own world. I love theatre at all levels from farce through thriller to drama, for each of us has many moods and theatre rightly reflects them all, but I was in search of something beyond words, a theatre of images. Here was a form of theatre capable of affecting and profoundly changing people's perceptions and, therefore, their whole lives. Above all, I recognized that in her work Martha Graham was rediscovering the religious and sacred origins of theatre. When, in *Errand into the Maze*

Graham as Ariadne came face to face with the feared Minotaur, she was doing battle with the darkness that is also our darkness; coming to terms with it on our behalf, and emerging triumph- antly from the maze that is also our maze. In doing this she was enacting the sacred mysteries of our own times, the ritualistic purgation of our interior darkness, and the revelation of our innermost selves. She told me how she came to create that particular work. The company was touring the East and, travelling in a DC6 which could not fly at an altitude greater than 9000 feet, they had to negotiate a pass, in a blinding snowstorm, through mountains 19,000 feet high. The dancers were terrified, 'but I sat and went into the heart of the terror by creating in my head the ballet of *Errand into the Maze*. I was able to get through the entire work three times and then I felt calm. The aim of the work then became to share that experience with others.'

I went to almost every performance during that first London season, taking notes and seeing each of the works several times. At my first meeting with Martha Graham she turned, laughing, to her companion, Leroy Leatherman, and said of one work, *Dark Meadow*, 'He understands it all. We don't have to explain it to him!' So many people had hated *Dark Meadow*. 'People are afraid of the unknown,' she commented. When I talked about the sense of space, of earth and sky, in *Appalachian Spring*, and the first prostration to the soil of the two protagonists, the young husband and wife, after which they turn to the sky and send out a kiss to the universe, she replied, 'In the end we have to get back to these simple things, for they are what remain in the end. Civilization changes, differs, but the earth, the sky, the elements, they remain.' When I spoke of the sense of peace in this work, she added, 'But that peace can come only from suffering – provided one is prepared to abandon oneself.'

'And that,' I observed, 'is the message of *Dark Meadow*.'

At that same meeting Martha Graham spoke of the great actress Eleonora Duse and described the first time she saw her. 'Goodness, how long ago! I was appearing in the Greenwich Town Follies. I shall never forget where my seat was that afternoon. I only saw her once but it was unforgettable. She was old, ridden with disease, at the end of her life – but she held me. I remember how she slipped a shawl off her shoulders and clenched her hand and in that simple gesture there was everything of agony and acceptance. One was moved because she had – vision.

'One is a servant of the public. One has something to give them. And every performance must be approached in a spirit of dedication. One has a great responsibility. You can never tell what effect you are going to have. I remember once, giving a performance of my solo, *Lamentation*, the study of a woman in grief, and afterwards a woman came round to see me and said, "I want to thank you for tonight. Last week I saw both my children killed in an automobile accident and I was unable to weep. Tonight, for the first time, I have been able to weep – because you have shown me that there can be dignity in suffering."

'I always tell my students that *how* they work, the state of mind in which they approach a performance, is what determines whether or not they are good performers. You must be able to empty yourself completely into the rôle on stage. Yet in performance you must never reach the utmost peak of the movement. Dancing is a state of becoming. The Balinese dance to restore the cosmic balance of the world. You must not force your weight one way or the other, or you will tip the scale. If you force your movement to the end of your ability there will be nothing left. The sense of infinite freedom and continuity will be lost.'

We were seated on a low divan in her theatre dressing room. With upright back, hands clasped formally in her lap, she was wearing a black kimono over a white costume, having that evening performed just one work, *Letter to the World*, in which she portrayed Emily Dickinson. There seemed about us, as we talked, a great stillness, a sense of calm, as of two people reaching out to each other, resting for a moment in one another. I know that this sounds presumptuous, but it is what I felt at the time and what I still recall.

'In my work,' she went on, 'I have always sought to reveal an image of man in his struggle for wholeness, for what you might call God's idea of man rather than his own idea of himself. I should like you to write to me from time to time in New York. I should like to hear from you and what you are doing. You have vision and that is rare. One likes to know what happens to it.' She smiled at me with pleasure. 'You have said and written such wonderful things. You have given me so much.'

As I rose to go I said, 'You must be very tired.'

'Not so tired tonight, because I have only had to dance once. One is only tired when one has messed things up for oneself.' She paused and smiled. 'Sometimes people can give one peace – and you have given me peace.' She inclined her head and turned the flat of her palm in a Japanese gesture of gratitude.

After the final performance of that season, when I was taken past the long queue of people waiting all up the stairs to speak to her, and hurried through into her presence, she embraced me. 'You'll write?' She was laughing, relaxed, contented, happy. 'You look like a Brontë tonight!' she teased me.

In 1964 we met again, both on the first night of her triumphant return season, and subsequently at a special luncheon given in her honour at the American Embassy. She was the only woman present, and the twenty-one guests included Sir Frederick Ashton, Sir John Gielgud, Sir David Webster, various English ballet critics, and Robert Cohan and Bertram Ross, two leading dancers from the company. Afterwards we posed for a group photograph in the Embassy foyer against a background of fountains. Then someone came up to me: 'Miss Graham would like to be photographed with you.'

I held her hand and gazed at her. 'You should look at the camera!' she said, smiling, but I didn't, and turning to her I said, 'You have given me so much. I want to thank you. I want you to know that I have found my way.'

There are moments in one's life for which few words can be found. It is, after all, a rare experience to meet so powerful an influence in the theatre as Martha Graham, to absorb and integrate it into oneself, and then, a decade later, to meet again and be able to acknowledge such a debt. With this meeting and with that moment in which I held her hand I felt that I had come full circle.

But in the spring of 1954 London was disturbed. There were many who hated her work, or ridiculed it, because it cut so keenly to the bone. As Craig Barton, a great friend of Miss Graham's, wrote to me at the time,

> Martha's dancing is about something. It does not entertain or provide distraction. One sees a visual masterpiece in which the dancers move in a masterly and special way, but the reaction of the

spectator moves on to another plane of inner revelation, of excited unrest. Even a lyrical abstraction like *Diversion of Angels* has a radiation that shakes one's interior. One has had a serious experience.

In the Invocation to *The Conference of Birds*, a poem by the twelfth century Persian Sufi poet, the reader is asked, 'Do you think it will be easy to arrive at a knowledge of spiritual things? It means no less than to die to everything. My friends, I wish to repeat my discourse to you day and night so that you should not cease for a moment too long to set out in quest of the Truth.' The quest, of course, is endless. It is renewed every day, taking many forms, leading us along paths we could not have foreseen and which we would not have chosen for ourselves. It is a quest that continues to the end and beyond. In 1955 that quest led me, via Martha Graham, to New York where I joined the faculty of the Julliard School of Music. Here I was given a studio, a group of dancers, singers, musicians and one composer, and invited to experiment with the integration of music, dance and drama.

It would lead to meetings with other key figures in the world of modern dance: Doris Humphrey, Louis Horst, José Limon, John Martin, Anthony Tudor, Walter Terry, Pearl Lang, Alwin Nikolais and Murray Louis, as well as encounters with Robert Frost, Eileen Garrett and others. This was to be a year in which foundations were laid for work that only now is beginning to come to fruition.

That was the real world: I have touched it once,
And now shall know it always. But the lie,
The Maze, the wild-wood waste of falsehood. Roads
That run and run and never reach an end,
Embowered in error – I'd be prisoned there
But that my soul has birdwings to fly free.

Edwin Muir

2

The Voyage Out

'What novels do you write?' she asked.
  'I want to write a novel about Silence,' he said; 'the things people don't say. But the difficulty is immense.'

Virginia Woolf, *The Voyage Out*

Before flying out to New York in the autumn of 1955 I had drawn up an elaborate and detailed schedule of work for the whole year which at the last minute I threw away. I realized that if the work was to be truly experimental then there could be no map of territory that was, as yet, uncharted. I knew only that, as a director, I had a desire to experiment with the materials of my craft, to juxtapose bodies, voices, sounds, movements, dance, shapes and colours. I called the course 'Theatre of Imagination'. At my first meeting with the students I told them that the main purpose of the year was to give them a personal experience of drama, rather than an intellectual exploration, enabling them to find within themselves the *why* of theatre, and to create an original work that would speak for them both as individuals and as a group. How we were to achieve this I did not yet know. All I knew was that we would have to proceed by trial and error, class by class, exercising a considerable amount of faith in the creative principle to declare itself and point the way. First, however, out of a group of varying backgrounds, ages, experience and expectations, we had to forge a unity so that we could arrive at a point where we could feel free to reveal ourselves without fear.

One of the music students subsequently recorded her impressions of that first day.

The Registrar had placed me in this class because it was the only thing that fitted into my schedule and, as he did so, he muttered something about its dealing with the beginnings of theatre. His veiled references to the scope of the course led me to believe that it was a staid theatrical course.

When I entered Room 201 for the first time I saw a red-headed young man wearing a blue sweat shirt, blue jeans and – barefooted. I was somewhat astonished to learn that he was the teacher, since he was the first teacher I had ever seen without shoes. In the following hour and twenty minutes he told us that we would also be expected to remove our footgear for the rest of the year in his class. The entire session was quite a shock.

For a long time rumours spread of the barefoot class that sat in the dark or performed strange exercises with rubber babies, birds in cages, and wooden hoops, screaming and laughing. I was unofficially known as 'The Barefoot Contessa'. Sometimes the students were given large sheets of paper onto which they would splash bright-coloured paints; at other times they were taken out along the Hudson River and encouraged to jump, run and turn cartwheels, like children; all were attempts to release their own creativity. There were times I despaired as much of myself as of them. If they were often in the dark it was because I, in-experienced as a teacher, was myself in the dark. The process of getting to know each other was also very painful. That they were American and I British seemed often to get in the way: you can speak the same language and yet not communicate. Then, too, I worked instinctively in terms of symbol and archetype, while they argued always in terms of: What use will this be to me as a musician, a dancer? In fact I had as much to learn from them as they from me, but this is always true in a creative teaching situation. I found that I could not assume the normal – to me – references to folklore, Bible, fairy tale, legend and history. In addition they remained stubbornly and rigidly on the defensive, distrustful of spontaneity, and afraid of opening themselves to the experimental and unpredictable. (It is important to remember that these were the 1950s and not the freer, more open, 1960s.) Finally, of course, the very nature of the work was bound to arouse deep resistance, and for a time there was near-chaos: mutinies, calculated insolence and fierce, destructive arguments that sought to undermine me. Sometimes classes petered out and I had to dismiss everyone. Only the support of Doris Humphrey*– whose rehearsals I attended regularly – and Anthony Tudor enabled me to persevere. Eventually I went to William Schumann, the composer-President of Julliard at the time, and insisted that the disruptive and unwilling members of the group be removed since they were deriving no benefit from the class and were merely preventing the rest from achieving anything constructive – of course I now know that in any experimental work such an initial period of upheaval and resistance is to be expected.

So it was that with the New Year of 1956 came the first signs of spontaneous creative activity. Once the unruly elements had been thrown out, and the group had been reduced to a more manageable ten (at that time I knew nothing about group dynamics and the need in any intensive work for a group not larger than twelve), the real work began. I set each student an individual assignment: to create an original work of theatre by drawing upon some inner experience – fantasy, fear, desire or conflict. I took as our definition of theatre the objectification, through the medium of theatre, of an inner reality.

The histrionic is a natural tendency. When we are happy we sing and dance; when frustrated we stamp and swear; when in pain we rock and moan. It is the performance of these actions that, in dramatizing the mood, affords relief. But the histrionic is not necessarily art, which implies a form and shape in time and space, and the necessity of communicating its content to others so that it can become a shared experience. What is originally subjective must be made objective through technique.

I now began to work with the students individually, outside the hours of the regular class. Each would bring me the theme on which they were working and together we would try to find its inherent form. I insisted always on one thing: that however abstract the work might become in the final process, it had to have a firm basis in reality. The abstract has to grow from the concrete, the universal from the particular. So if the theme were that of feeling lost, we might begin with the experience of being

*Doris Humphrey and Anthony Tudor were on the teaching staff of the Julliard School of Music's Dance Department. Martha Graham, and Doris Humphrey, another leading pioneer of modern dance, and Anthony Tudor, distinguished choreographer were on the staff of the Julliard.

lost as a child, or the panic of not being able to find the right train
on the subway late at night; fear of being lost, *where*? In a
labyrinth? In the dark? No attitudinizing or vague expressions of
emotion were permitted. Seated in a corner with a drum, I would
try to follow and assist with a drumbeat whatever was being
improvised. The beat was there to act as an inner pulse, no more.
For as long as need be I would continue to beat the drum
monotonously and the student would sit, lie or stand, until
eventually something quite spontaneous and unforeseen would
begin to happen. It might be at first quite a small movement but
that would lead on to the next, and then the improvisation would
be under way. It was out of such improvisations that the works
grew. Even now, though I use specific exercises that have evolved
over the years to release unconscious material, the improvisation
comes first. The actor, the individual, is his own creator. Once a
theme has been released and a central image found, each
successive improvisation becomes a fresh exploration of this
theme, a further development of the central image, until gradually, layer by layer, detail by detail, the final work is crystallized.
    Such a way of working involved certain dangers, certain
responsibilities on my part, since I was not a trained therapist. In
order to minimize the degree of emotional involvement on my
part I used to avoid personal comment on the content of the
work, discussing it solely on a professional basis in terms of its
dramatic and kinetic shape. All that I asked of the students was
that the end result be shaped and pruned down to its barest
essentials, with every phrase, movement and sound ruthlessly
rehearsed, and nothing left to improvisation in performance.
Slowly I realized that what we were trying to do was expressed in
Virginia Woolf's first novel, *The Voyage Out*, in which a writer is
asked what kind of books he wants to write and he replies that
they would be books about silence – about the things which
people do not say.
    Similarly Martha Graham has said, 'There is a necessity for
movement when words are inadequate. The basis of all dancing is
something deep within you.' For Graham each of her works has
been a point of departure for her questing spirit. She has always
been The One Who Seeks (the name of her protagonist in *Dark
Meadow*), delving below the surface for the 'why' underneath;
agreeing with Picasso that a portrait should not be simply a

physical likeness but rather a psychological or spiritual likeness, what she has described as 'a graph of the heart, a blueprint of the soul'. But this kind of creativity calls for great courage. Graham once told the story of a very beautiful and talented dancer whom she invited to create a dance for herself. The girl said she had seen the fear and pain on Graham's face when she was choreographing and that if this was part of it then she wanted none of it. And so she had none of it but, as Graham added gravely, she never created the dance. Each one of us has a seed of life within us which must create the form or body that will be its inevitable fulfilment, like those multi-hued seashells, each one of which is unique, which the sea animal creates to house most perfectly its own particular spark of life. Each one of us has our own myth to live, our own song to sing, our own tale to tell, and if we are to fulfil it we need the same courage that the professional artist requires. The spiritual process exactly mirrors the creative one.

Each of the students produced a number of short pieces, many of which were discarded (another important creative and spiritual principle: 'You have to live by shedding,' wrote Robert Frost) or grew into something else. Some of the group were more prolific than others, and one or two achieved very little. It was at this point that I myself performed two improvisations within the group. Up till then I had carefully avoided seeming to demonstrate anything in order to leave them free to follow their own creative instincts. Now, however, by being unafraid to reveal myself I was encouraging them to do likewise, but always one student sat outside with the drum in my place.

As one of them said at the time, 'At first it was terribly difficult to do my solo in class because it was *me* speaking and it scared me, but you helped me realize that only by doing something terribly personal and basic could I ever arrive at an experience of original theatre.' At first this student, Carolyn Gracey, had attempted to dramatize her sense of loss on the death, some months earlier, of a much-loved teacher, but each time the result had been forced, unreal, bound by naturalism. How her solo emerged she herself later described:

In working on my individual pieces I learned through experience that we cannot work on a subject unless we can look at it objectively. This I found out when doing my piece on Mr B's death. The solo on 'God' which followed this and which I finally performed, was the result of my being deeply disturbed by a class discussion in which several of the students attacked the idea of the existence of God, in consequence of which I spent a tortured night, unable to sleep. The next day when I met with you I was so uptight that when you asked me to relax and just let something come, I became even more tense until, suddenly, the conflict and trouble in my mind spilled over into the improvisation.

Her work was entitled *From Forth This Circle*. She began seated on the floor inside a wooden hoop, rocking forwards and backwards in an agitated manner. Slowly the words 'No God!' were articulated, being repeated over and over with monotonous persistence. She picked up the hoop, wrestling with it, becoming trapped inside it as though she were in a bottomless pit. Repeatedly she cried out the words of her private terror until, at the climax, she gave a cry of despair and collapsed. Slowly she opened her eyes and, gazing at the hoop encircling her, touched it gently with her fingers, quietly singing, like a child's nursery rhyme, the words: 'My circle is my God. My God is my circle.' Lifting the hoop, she stood up, raising it above her head like a spinning disc or halo of light, singing out with an intense joy: '*My circle encompasses me!*'

The simplicity of this short work – which lasted about seven minutes – the intensity of its emotion, its crystallization of a real and recognizable human dilemma, recalled those delicate, fragmentary poems of Emily Dickinson, each one a minute graph of a mood and of her own inner spiritual development, as in

> Who has not found the heaven below
> Will fail of it above.
> God's residence is next to mine,
> His furniture is love.

or

> I felt a funeral in my brain,
> And mourners, to and fro,
> Kept treading, treading, till it seemed
> That sense was breaking through.

And when they all were seated,
A service like a drum
Kept beating, beating, till I thought
My mind was going numb.

And then I heard them lift a box,
And creak across my soul
With those same boots of lead, again.
Then space began to tell

As all the heavens were a bell,
And Being but an ear,
And I and silence some strange race,
Wrecked solitary, here.

Patience, sympathy, tact, objectivity and an imaginative identification with each student were required from me. I remember vividly the day when one dancer, Sandra Goldberg, did an improvisation lasting over an hour. Up to that moment she had always broken off before reaching the climax of an exercise, with the result that nothing was ever finished. This distressed her and it became important that she should complete something. On this particular morning she began to create a ritual involving a flight of steps, a lamp, a hoop, a spear, a length of white rope and an African drum that was hollow at one end. Perhaps of all the works performed in the final demonstration this was the most haunting, and on the strength of it Pearl Lang invited the dancer to join her modern dance company.

The work began with the girl removing from her side the spear with which plainly she had been wounded, and reaching towards the light – as to the sun – for strength and healing. There followed a journey through the hoop and the discovery of the drum as something that could contain objects. Returning to base, she placed the drum and spear in the centre of the wooden hoop. A second foray revealed the white rope, while the final expedition brought her to the Sacred Mountain of Three Steps, to which she now dragged her possessions. Taking the white rope she wove across the hoop the pattern of a star. Lifting the spear, she circled the Mountain in a dance that sought to exorcise her fear of the spear. Finally she plunged the spear into the starred hoop and, on removing it, saw it no longer as a remembered pain but as a weapon in her own hands which she could use. Now she took the hoop and lowered it over her body like a snake shedding a skin (shedding the pain of the remembered wound); finally, raising the drum to her head like a crown and holding the spear like a sceptre in the other hand, she walked out of the landscape. The work was entitled *From Forth This Landscape*.

This work was strangely compelling, partly because of the authority with which it had been conceived, designed and performed, and also because it was so clearly a modern ritual, an exorcism of subconscious fears, a search for identity, pointing the way towards a new maturity in the image of the woman-queen-warrior emerging from the chrysalis. Years later I was to discover this poem by Emily Dickinson which describes exactly this journey of individuation, that process whereby an individual discovers her identity.

> I'm ceded, I've stopped being theirs;
> The name they dropped upon my face
> With water in the country church,
> Is finished using now,
> And they can put it with my dolls,
> My childhood, and the string of spools
> I've finished threading too.
>
> Baptised before without the choice
> But this time, consciously, of grace
> Unto supremest name,
> Called to my full, the crescent dropped,
> Existence's whole arc filled up
> With one small diadem.
>
> My second rank, too small the first,
> Crowned, crowing on my father's breast,
> A half-unconscious queen;
> But this time, adequate, erect,
> With will to choose or to reject,
> And I choose – just a throne.

Of the year's work Sandra Goldberg later wrote,

It was a journey. Not through books to acquire factual material but through ourselves. With the aim to find within ourselves the heart of theatre. The first part of the year was difficult because this was the soul-seeking journey, the search blindly, the discovery within ourselves of things we had never realised were there.

Our first problem was to lose our inhibitions, to be willing to seek for what we were searching. This caused much conflict and tension for not everyone was willing to free themselves. Which I feel was foolish. There was nothing to fear, for where there is freedom there is knowledge, and where there is knowledge there is freedom. When we finally did reach a point where we felt the desire to express and communicate something from within ourselves, I was surprised at myself and at others for we were finding things within us that could be used for theatre.

After rehearsing my piece there was the problem of intensifying or emphasizing it in order to enable it to be transmitted in terms of dynamics, rhythm, tempo, its pattern in space. Finally I experienced performing something that was personal to me and yet objectified enough to be theatrical. Thank you so much for your guidance through this journey.

When all the works came to be performed before an invited audience, there were those who were shocked or angry, others who were bored or mildly interested, some who laughed, and some who were absorbed and fascinated. As Bruce Marks, later a leading dancer with the American Ballet Theatre, but at the time a principal in Pearl Lang's company, said to me years afterwards, 'At that time there was no one talking like you, saying the things you were saying. They just didn't understand.'

It was a long time before I myself was able to assess the exact value of what had been achieved. I only knew that this was the direction the work had taken and that I had gone with it, but it laid the foundations of my later work in ritual. What meant most to me on that particular evening was to hear Pearl Lang, whom I had first seen as a leading dancer in the Martha Graham company in London, say, 'You have given me fresh hope. You have achieved so much. We need you here. We need you here and at Yale. We need you more for dancers than for actors. If we asked you, would you stay?'

As a result of my work at the Julliard I was asked by Ted Shawn to give a course at Denishawn, the home of modern dance, and invited by Alwin Nikolais to start a school of drama, eventually with its own professional company, at the Henry Street Playhouse where he was then working with his own dance company. However, I felt that there would be time for further experimentation later. The days of my apprenticeship were at an end, and I returned to England.

God be with you strongly. May He lead you into the deepest
solitude and be a circle of fire round you. Always.

(*Meinrad Craighead to James Roose-Evans on the eve of
his ordination.*)

3

The Return Journey

It was in the late 1950s that a school of meditation was set up in
London which promoted a simple form of meditation based upon
a word mantra, similar to the one then beginning to be taught by
the Maharishi in India. I enrolled, was given my mantra (one of
the sacred names of God and not a meaningless word, as so many
have claimed). I responded at once to this form of meditation and
began to 'hear the words of secret silence'*. Of course, all such
beginnings are euphoric and difficulties must be experienced after
a while, but the way was complicated by the fact that each week
the voluntary counsellors kept changing. It was rare to get the
same person twice running, and each often appeared to be giving
contradictory instruction. I also began to find a conflict between
my desire to follow the mantra I had been given and a desire to be
responding to the Christ within – even though, at that time, I had
ceased going to church.

In India the sacred names of God, as used in meditation, have
great richness in them, but a Westerner needs a skilled master if he
is to employ these techniques. Thomas Merton† considered that,
of all the paths to a deeper spirituality, the one most suited to a
Westerner seeking to attain a higher level of religious consciousness within the Christian context was probably Zen because it is
not a religion, nor a philosophy, nor a form of mysticism, but

*'I hear the words of secret silence' – words from an unpublished poem by the
calligraphic artist John Rowlands Pritchard.
†Thomas Merton: a convert to Catholicism, he became a Cistercian monk, entering
Gethsemani Monastery in Kentucky at the age of 26. He died in 1968. He became the
leading contemplative voice of the twentieth century, and the first American writer to
make a significant statement about spirituality.

primarily a way of seeing, of remaining open to experience. Certainly I experienced this for myself once I stopped going to the school of meditation and began to persevere on my own. Soon other teachers appeared to guide and assist, as they always do.

This search for a deeper spiritual centre and life of prayer was happening at one of the fullest and most demanding periods of my life. Only someone who has started an enterprise from scratch, without any finance, can really understand the unremitting slog of a shoestring organization. The Hampstead Theatre began from nothing, and it was seven lean years before it received regular grant aid from the Arts Council, so that in those early years it struggled from one financial crisis to another. But though we were poor, we generated a whirlpool of enthusiasm and energy. In these days of still heavily subsidized theatre, with an established fringe (the phrase 'fringe theatre' had not even been coined), it has to be remembered that outside the West End the Hampstead Theatre was then the only London-based small theatre with its own premises; it was the successor to the Everyman Theatre in the 1920s, and the Embassy Theatre in the 1940s.

The Hampstead Theatre began in a church hall in September 1959 and had its first successful year there next to the Everyman Cinema. There followed an abortive year while I tried to set up a theatre-in-a-pub, designed by Anthony Gough who was to design the present theatre at Swiss Cottage. Again, had not the authorities intervened and insisted on expensive fire escapes we would have been the first theatre-in-a-pub, now a familiar part of the London theatre scene. The following year Hampstead Borough Council decided to build a small prefabricated theatre at Swiss Cottage, designed to last ten years. This was opened in December 1962. A few of us worked all hours, rehearsing, manning the box office, addressing envelopes, tramping the neighbourhood delivering leaflets – and in the process learning much about the psychology of letterboxes. Snow fell heavily during the opening production, in what proved to be one of the worst winters since 1947. We had no money to advertise or publicize, and because there was then no established fringe it meant that our first nights invariably clashed with first nights in

the West End, with the result that we often got no critics: no
critics meant no reviews; no reviews meant no audiences.

Within a few months we reached a stage of financial crisis, and
dramatic headlines announced our imminent closure. I wrote to
all the critics begging them to cover our productions, arguing the
case that London needed such a small chamber theatre where new
work could be tested. Writing to Harold Hobson, drama critic of
The Sunday Times, I spelled it out in large letters: 'WE NEED YOUR
SPACE!' I decided to revive Noël Coward's *Private Lives* (his first
great success, *The Vortex*, had been staged in the 1920s at the
Everyman Theatre) and I directed it not as a period piece but in a
contemporary setting. Harold Hobson came to the first night, as
did Bernard Levin and other critics. Their rave notices caused
Noël Coward to fly in from Australia for a special performance.
The production transferred to the Duke of York's Theatre in the
West End where it ran for over a year, resulting in what Coward
later referred to as 'Dad's Renaissance'. Simultaneous with this,
Max Rayne (later to be knighted, then made a peer, and become
chairman of the National Theatre) came to our rescue, clearing
all debts, giving sound practical advice, printing a handsome
brochure about the theatre, and organizing a gala performance of
Private Lives to which the famous and the fashionable were
invited. Suddenly everyone was talking about the Hampstead
Theatre. *Private Lives* was followed by Laurie Lee's *Cider with
Rosie* and, amidst acclaim from Bernard Levin, Clive Barnes,
Robert Kee, Harold Hobson and others, transferred to the West
End. That season also included Marguerite Duras's *The Square*,
and the 1500-year-old Sanskrit classic *The Little Clay Cart*.

Each season had a theme. During the Living Theatre season,
devoted to documentary theatre, and predating Peter Brook's *US*
at the Aldwych, a white bicycle stood on the roof of the theatre,
the symbol of the Provos in Amsterdam, while the poster depicted
the image of Bernard de Vries, leader of the Dutch Provos, racing
through the streets bearing a lighted torch. The season opened –
and nearly closed – with Heinz Kipphardt's controversial play *In
the Matter of J. Robert Oppenheimer*, directed by Peter Coe. No
one else would risk staging or even publishing it because of the
threat of writs for libel from the real-life characters depicted in it.
In the end none were served, the production transferred to the

West End and subsequently the text was published by Methuen. It was followed by *Letters from an Eastern Front*; Michael Hastings's *The Silence of Lee Harvey Oswald*; and Patrick Garland's brilliant adaptation and production of John Aubrey's *Brief Lives*; the season ended with *An Evening with Malcolm Muggeridge*. Also staged in these first years were plays by John McGrath (two), David Hare, Colin Spencer (two), John Bowen (two), James Kennaway, Wole Soyinka, Athol Fugard, Tennessee Williams (world première of *The Two Character Play*, later called *Outcry!*), Andrew Sinclair, Jack Pulman, Clive Exton, Peter Terson, Howard Sackler, Barry Bermange (three), Giles Cooper, Le Roi Jones, Frank Marcus, John Antrobus, Kenneth Ross (two), Roger Milner and many more. There were Sunday night shows, a Poetry Series, exhibitions in the foyer, and al fresco parties on the patio throughout the summer after every first night.

After ten years, the first seven without subsidy, I and everyone else were still being paid a pittance. I had no assistant, there was one secretary, no press representative and no script readers. John Mortimer, backed by Dame Peggy Ashcroft, Sir Michael Redgrave, Dame Sybil Thorndike and others, made an impassioned appeal for proper funding. The strain of mounting eight to ten productions a year created a feeling of being trapped on a conveyor belt and yet, as we entered our second decade, it seemed to me important that, rather than rest on our laurels, or collapse from weariness, or seek greater financial gain elsewhere, we should take time out to research. I therefore set up an experimental wing called Stage Two and launched an appeal for funds that would enable us to rent premises and engage a small company of actors.

Apart from Nancy Meckler's The Freehold, Stage Two was the only other experimental company in England at the time and, unlike The Freehold, had no Arts Council backing. I raised enough money for one year, and after nine months the company presented its first works which were highly praised by, among others, Ronald Bryden in *The Observer*, Harold Hobson in *The Sunday Times*, B. A. Young in *The Financial Times*, Nicholas de Jongh in *The Guardian*, Oleg Kerensky in *The Daily Mail* and J. C. Trewin in *The Illustrated London News*. In spite of this the Arts Council, on the opinion of a single officer, turned down an application for a grant. Without further financial aid the venture closed. The seeds of that one year's work, however, have gone on growing in workshops, primarily in America, and have led me finally into the area of ritual.

In his journal Isamu Noguchi, the American-Japanese stage designer and sculptor, writes, 'I wanted other means of communication – to find a way of sculpture that was humanly meaningful without being realistic, at once abstract and relevant – I wanted to find out what sculpture was fundamentally about. I felt it had become captive, like the other arts, to coterie points of view.' If one substitutes for the word 'sculpture' the word 'theatre', this sums up my own feelings and reflections during the latter half of the 1960s. Increasingly I came to see the importance of taking time out to search and research. It seemed to me then, and still does, that the drama in England, like its Church, was merely repeating itself in varying styles of naturalism, and that it was being saturated with words: a cerebral theatre and a cerebral church.

It is not irrelevant to this autobiographical sketch that in 1965 I had resumed analysis with Dr Franz Elkisch. He asked me why I was returning to him. I replied that I was coming up to thirty-eight, that I felt worn out, as though I had already lived several lives, and ought to make a will. He laughed. His laughter on that occasion remains with me now. It was like that of a Zen master, dispelling the clouds of pomposity, of taking one's self too seriously. I also told him that I was aware of much more to give and to discover, aware also that it might be a time for new departures in my work. I am inclined to think that each decade, as it approaches, signals a need for change, and that the secret of ageing lies in remaining open to the Tao, the Way.

In her recent novel, *The Good Apprentice*, Iris Murdoch has this comment to make on the rôle of the therapist:

> God is a belief that at our deepest level we are known and loved, even there the rays can penetrate. But the therapist is not God, not even a priest or a sage, and must prompt the sufferer to heal himself through his own deities, and this involves finding them. How many souls there are who, encountering no good powers, are never healed at all . . . . Each person is different . . . the myth that heals is an individual work of art.

This is what Jung means when he refers to one's personal myth, which one must learn and live out. As the French Benedictine monk Father Henri le Saux (Abhishiktananda) has written: 'Surely a man is in need of some myth or other, in order to release in him that which would otherwise remain for ever buried deep down in his psyche?' For Abhishiktananda it was in the sacred mountain of Arunachala in the Himalayas that he found his myth: 'I have found here something which no other place . . . no other being has ever been able to give me.' It was his meeting in 1949 with Sri Ramana Maharshi, the great sage of South India, that led him to discover the sacred mountain of Arunachala, where for several long periods between 1952 and 1955 he lived as a hermit in its caves. Here he entered deeply into the experience of India's holymen and saints, and gained new insights into the mystery of Christ. Together with Father Jules Monchanin, Dom Bede Griffiths, Thomas Merton and others, he did much to break down the barriers of prejudice and misunderstanding that separate the followers of different religious traditions.

My analysis continued afresh, at a deeper level, until the day when I recounted a particular dream. At that point Dr Elkisch said, 'You have found your personal myth. My task is ended. You no longer need me.' From that moment our relationship changed. We were no longer analyst and patient, but two friends, Franz and Jimmie, who, in meetings that went on until shortly before his death, would talk and occasionally share each other's dreams.

In 1973 I resigned from the Hampstead Theatre in order to develop a freelance career as a director and writer, travelling to America, Greece, Denmark, Africa and other parts of the world. They were lean and difficult years. Then in 1980, while working in America, I was given a slim volume of letters, entitled *84 Charing Cross Road*, by Helene Hanff. I acquired the stage rights, adapted it, and in 1981 directed it in a try-out production at the Salisbury Playhouse in Wiltshire. It was so successful that it transferred to the West End, starring Rosemary Leach and David Swift, where it ran for eighteen months at the Ambassadors Theatre. During that run I went to New York to direct it on Broadway where, with Ellen Burstyn and Joseph Maher in the leading rôles, it ran for three months. Both in London and New York it won various awards: Best Actress, Best Actor, Best Play and Best Director. Later, in 1986, it was made into a film with Anne Bancroft and Anthony Hopkins.

But in that summer of 1981, while the many events of this outward journey were unfolding, another inner journey was nearing its completion. It resulted in my being ordained deacon early in the morning of St David's Day at Glasshampton Monastery in Worcestershire, surrounded only by the brethren. Then, four months later, and a week before the start of rehearsals for 84 *Charing Cross Road*, I was ordained priest in Hereford Cathedral. It was some four years earlier that a priest friend had said to me one evening in my house in Wales, 'James, why don't you take Orders?' I had thought about that question deeply but could not see how it was possible, for I knew I was not called to give up my work in the theatre and become a parish priest. Some months later I was in Cambridge, lecturing, when I attended the early Eucharist on Whit Sunday at Christ's College, where a friend, Bruce Addison, was chaplain. During his address he asked this simple question: What will you do for the Lord? And I thought – ordination. I had a talk with him and it was he who explained to me about the non-stipendiary ministry, a scheme launched by the Anglican Church in 1963 and whose numbers include farmers, doctors, teachers, financiers, actors and others, each of whom earns his living like other people, and each of whom exercises a particular ministry.

It was also about this time that I had a dream which clearly signalled that a major change was approaching. All important dreams herald a period of upheaval and change. Such dreams are not like puzzles capable of a quick solution and then, once solved, of no further use; they have, rather, an enigmatic quality like the statements of an oracle, capable of many levels of interpretation, and of lasting a lifetime. I was fortunate that I was able to share this dream with Franz Elkisch shortly before his death, and discuss with him this call to the priesthood. In the dream I was giving a lecture about the creative process and explaining how always out of *nothing*, whether it be a blank sheet of paper for the writer, a blank canvas for the artist, or a block of stone for the scultor, *something* is created. As I spoke I was projecting onto a blank screen various images from a slide projector. Then the screen dissolved into a glass window through which the sky could be seen. From far away, out of space, and travelling towards me, I could see a shape that I recognized, even within the dream, as being a deeper aspect of my self. The question with which I was faced was: Do I hurl myself through the glass and go to meet it, even if I wound myself in the process? Or do I sit here, waiting for it to draw nearer? Franz Elkisch urged me to wait, saying that to try and anticipate what was already in motion, to make it happen sooner, would be the act of my ego and only result in harm, as the dream indicated. My task was to wait in patience for this aspect of the Self to reveal its purpose. Long afterwards, while at Glasshampton Monastery, I was to come across these words by Father Gilbert Shaw:

Look well, O soul, upon thyself
Lest spiritual ambition
Should mislead and blind thee
To thy essential task –
To wait in quietness:
To knock and persevere in humble faith.
Knock thou in love, nor fail to keep thy place before the door –
That when Christ wills – and not before –
He shall open unto thee the treasures of his love.

The path to ordination did indeed unfold of its own accord, although I had many doubts from the start. 'What a relief!' commented Canon Murray Irvine, my director of ordinands. 'Most people think they are God's gift to the Church.' I also knew that if any element of seeking were to be found on my part that would have to be a reason for stepping aside, for this was not a goal to be achieved. For a long time I wrestled with the question: Why ordination? At one level all Christians are ministers and share in a common priesthood. It was quite clear that I already had a ministry in my work, which found its clearest expression when exploring archetypal material in my workshops; or in my children's books, which attempt to deal with the religious quest; as well as in my everyday relationships and encounters. All of this was already flowing from a centre of prayer and the daily recital of the Office. During this period of doubt and questioning I wrote in my journal:

I know that with ordination a subtle shifting of attitudes will take
place and that, increasingly, more opportunities will be revealed,
and a greater burden be laid on me. I have an awareness of gifts as
yet untapped within myself and which, in this second half of my
life, are waiting to be harvested. I am not moving away from the
theatre or writing but rather, with ordination, these gifts will be
enhanced and woven into a richer pattern. If I am asked precisely
how I see my ministry, I have to reply: I do not yet know. I cannot
give a simple answer and say that it is to do this or that. In so far as I
can discern an emerging pattern it will be to act as a bridge between
opposites, and to be in myself such a bridge.

Ordination, of course, is a sacrament, 'an outward sign of
inward grace'. At the moment of laying on of hands a power is
transmitted. Thereafter a priest lives not for himself alone. 'From
tomorrow your lives will be different,' pronounced the Bishop of
Hereford during his solemn charge on the night before my
ordination, a night during which I endured the most violent and
bloody nightmares. 'You will be leaping into a void. Until you
have made the leap you cannot know what sacrifices and demands
will be asked of you. You cannot turn back. Before, life was easier,
your own. But in the void are God's arms. You will leap into
them, and he will never ask of you anything for which he has not
prepared you, and for which he will not give you the strength.'
    After I had been accepted by the Bishop of Hereford as a
candidate for ordination I was sent off to Glasshampton
Monastery to be interviewed by the Guardian, Brother Alban,
SSF. In almost the last conversation I had with Franz Elkisch he
had counselled: 'Don't let them send you to a theological college;
they will only try and brainwash you.' When, therefore, the
Bishop asked me what form of training I envisaged for the
ministry, I replied that I was in search of a Zen-like preparation of
prayer, study and work. He did not bat an eyelid, but then, of
course, he had been alerted, and given the matter long and careful
thought. 'I am sending you to Glasshampton Monastery to see
Brother Alban there who is the Guardian. It is the contemplative
house for the Society of St Francis, and all the brethren have to
spend some months there. If he can devise a form of training for
you, then I will accept that.'
    High on a hill a few miles outside Worcester, with the Welsh

and Malvern hills in the distance, stands a square red-brick building like a miniature barracks with a belfry and clock tower. The monastery of St Mary at the Cross, Glasshampton, is the former stables of a great house that no longer exists. They were converted into a monastic house by a remarkable and holy man, Father William, whose body rests in the cloister garth and whose story has been told by Geoffrey Curtis, C R. In his introduction to *William of Glasshampton* Brother Alban has written,

If it is God we seek, God we desire, we can find the real value of everything. But we have to find our way through a great deal of illusion for the love of God to be a reality for us – not an ideal, not a wistful hope, but a reality we know, even if in our foolishness we lose it over and over again, and have to return to the point where the vision is clear, unclouded and real. Then we see the value of God's gifts, the joy of being truly human, the splendour of the humanity which is ours. I do not think that any of us who have given our selves to life in a religious community would have done so if we had not had some inkling of where true value lies, which puts everything else in its proper perspective. That is the poverty of spirit which is blessed. That was the significance of the life Father William lived at Glasshampton.

We who are his successors, the Society of Saint Francis, are primarily an active community, though our life is meant to be, in one aspect, a dedication to this vision of truth so that we are available to it. There are very different life styles in our community; we do not all have the same particular concerns, but we have tried to put ourselves at God's disposal. Badly, it may be, inconsistently, unsteadily, but with some intention of living for God's sake. We are all damaged, we have our oddnesses and weaknesses as well as our particular strengths. We are fortunate if we know it, and take ourselves with our imperfections and angularities, as well as our strengths, to the God who accepts us and, because he does so, can help us to begin to accept ourselves. Not as we would like to be, but as we are, for it is from that point only that God can change us and make us grow. This we do not only for ourselves and for our own fulfilment, not only for each other, not only for those whom we seek to serve, but also as a witness that there is a God who calls us to his state of life. For ultimately we must say that while community life may be justified as useful for some, and that it does sometimes serve others, it would not have come into being without some sense that God does call us to it; that we do what we do in response to something that lies beyond us and which leads us on. This sense of being drawn by God may easily drop out of sight among the cares of caring, the agonies and depressions that overtake us all as we seek to bear those of others. That is why Glasshampton, with its atmosphere of prayer and reflection, has an important place in our community life, living in this environment which Father William's vision created, and which his spirit sustains.

At our first meeting, Brother Alban and I sat talking in his cell; then we went to the Chapel and knelt in silent prayer, side by side, for an hour. 'Come and be here whenever your work permits,' was his invitation. 'Follow the Spirit. When the time comes that you are ready for ordination you will know and I will know, and I will then tell the Bishop. That is all.' And so, over a period of nearly two years, Glasshampton became my centre, as it remains today; a place where gently, quietly, I learned many things. I have known it in full summer, in snow, during the time of my mother's death, in spring, summer again, and autumn into winter. There I have experienced peace, crisis and growth. I think it was Thomas Merton who wrote the following words which I copied into my journal one day at Glasshampton.

> My Lord, I have no idea where I am going, I do not see the road ahead of me, I cannot know for certain where it will end. Nor do I really know myself, and the fact that I am actually doing so. But I believe that the desire to please you does in fact please you. And I hope I have that desire in all that I am doing. I hope that I will never do anything apart from that desire. And I know that if I do this you will lead me by the right road even though I may know nothing about it. Therefore I will trust you always though I may seem to be lost and in the shadow of death, I will not fear, for you are ever with me and you will never leave me to face my perils alone.

After being accepted as a candidate for ordination, and by Brother Alban, I had to attend a three-day selection board for the ministry. I returned from it quite unconcerned about the result, yet I then developed an acute and painful depression that continued week after week. I was quite convinced that it had nothing to do with any anxiety as to whether or not I would be accepted for ordination, and so I did what I often do in such circumstances: I sat down and *drew* the situation. I began by drawing a picture of what I was feeling: at the bottom of a dried-up well. My pen sketched a deep vertical tunnel with a little stick figure at the bottom representing myself. At the well-head I drew a friar lowering a bucket from a winch which had a traditional tiled roof surmounted by a cross, rather like a sketch for a church. As I drew I saw that the bucket contained a single drop of moisture. Then at the bottom of the well I noticed a slight opening, and so I began to draw further, realizing that I had to make myself very small in order to crawl through this aperture. Beyond it lay a cave, and in that cave was an altar, and on that altar lay a seed, circular in shape like the Host at Mass. I knew then that it was my task to take the single drop of moisture from the bucket being lowered by the friar and water the seed. It was, of course, the seed of prayer which one must water daily. My pen began to sketch in slender tendrils growing out from the seed, climbing up through the dark earth towards the light, massing together to form first the roots, then the trunk and, finally, the branches of a mighty tree stretching up into the sky, and standing alongside the well-head where the friar was lowering the bucket with the drop of moisture that had set all this in motion. Inside the roots, trunk and branches I drew many faces which are the spirits of all creation – women, men and children – forming the living Tree of Christ.

> The tree of life my soul hath seen,
> Laden with fruit and always green:
> The trees of nature fruitless be
> Compared with Christ the apple tree.
>
> His beauty doth all things excel:
> By faith I know, but ne'er can tell
> The glory which I now can see
> In Jesus Christ the apple tree.
>
> For happiness I long have sought,
> And pleasure dearly I have bought:
> I missed of all, but now I see
> 'Tis found in Christ the apple tree.

I'm weary with my former toil,
Here I will sit and rest awhile:
Under the shadow I will be,
Of Jesus Christ the apple tree.

This fruit doth make my soul to thrive,
It keeps my dying faith alive,
Which makes my soul in haste to be
With Jesus Christ the apple tree.

From *Divine Hymns or Spiritual Songs*, compiled by Joshua Smith,
New Hampshire, 1784

With that drawing the depression lifted. The next day a letter
arrived, announcing that I had been accepted for ordination and
that my training might begin. As I had intuited, the depression
had had nothing to do with that decision. I continue to meditate
upon that drawing, which has a meaning over and beyond the
personal. It was my director of ordinands who said to me on our
first meeting, 'The Church has a great deal of dying to do', and in
this visualization one can see how the Church still has life in its
much neglected contemplative tradition through which the new
body of the Church will grow: 'The older order changeth,
yielding place to new.' I am but a small part of that process, and it
will not happen in one lifetime. It is not a matter of bureaucratic
change but of an inner growth which is sending out shoots deep
underground. It is what one friend has called 'The Waiting
Church', and what Dr Alec Vidler* has named 'the para-church',
which consists of small, unheralded groups living and working at
the fringe of the Church. Shortly before his death the writer and
critic Philip Toynbee wrote, 'My own conviction is that the
greatest intellectual vitality and moral hope now lies scattered
within the wild confusion of contemporary Christianity. I believe
that the way forward can only be by way of the Spirit.' Similarly
Karl Rahner, a Catholic theologian, saw the Church of the future
as the church of the little flock. Such Christian communities, he
says, will not be able to cover territorially large areas but, if they

*Dr Alec Vidler: Anglican priest and theologian. Born 1899, former Canon of St
George's Chapel, Windsor; author of many books, editor of *Theology*, Dean of King's
College, Cambridge. He also created with Malcolm Muggeridge a memorable
television series on St Paul.

are intensely devoted to their Lord, and, at the same time, outward looking, they will be effective weapons in God's hands. What is happening at the fringes of the Church is a quest for authenticity, a desire to discover and pay heed to the imperatives of one's own being, not to be satisfied with living by the often dubious standards applied by the establishment. As Dom Aelred Graham, OSB, of Ampleforth Abbey, has remarked, 'What is most called for is the exercise of powerful and intuitive minds without party allegiance that can reach behind the concepts of current theological controversies and illuminate what the religious quest is all about.'

How is it, some have asked, that I am now back within the Anglican fold and an ordained minister of it, while still practising my craft of theatre? How, some have challenged, can you be a member of a church that represents barely 1 per cent of the population and continues to dwindle? A church that is controlled by Parliament, a secular body, without any authority to enable it to say that the Church teaches this or that? A church where the form of the service, its liturgy, as well as the content of its teaching and preaching, varies from parish to parish? Even within one parish, as incumbent succeeds incumbent, the style and content can swing from High Anglican to Low Church and back again within one generation. What kind of Church is that? Especially to one who continues to draw daily from the Roman tradition, saying the Daily Office of that tradition, reciting the Rosary, and relating fundamentally to its teaching?

The answer lies in the fact that deep down I believe there is a Church beyond all Churches. As the Duchess of Malfi says in Webster's play of that name, 'I trow, sir, in the Eternal Church it will not be so.' As human beings we need tangible signs, we need structures, institutions and disciplines. In the end, however, each of us must follow our own conscience. This is what Father Conrad Pepler, OP, at Blackfriars, Oxford, taught me long ago. 'The catechism,' he explained, 'is there as a rough map for the faithful who need guidelines. It does not provide all the answers. It is important to know what the Church teaches and then, in the light of that, one must ultimately follow one's own conscience.' Even St Thomas Aquinas, perhaps the greatest intellect the Church has known, acknowledged the inadequacy of his great work, the *Summa Theologica*, in the light of the vision of truth that was granted to him at the end of his life. As a practising Catholic I was deeply struck by some words of Pope Pius XII spoken at a gathering of cardinals in Rome shortly before his death and reported by Christopher Hollis in *The Tablet*: 'The Roman Church must not seek to embrace the entire world. It must learn to accept that there are other faiths, other creeds, other temperaments.' They were remarkable words coming from him, and surely prophetic of what was to come through his successor, Pope John XXIII.

I cannot believe in the division of faiths, let alone the one Faith, nor of its Churches. There can be but one God under all, and one family of God. The truth shines with its own light. Each of us approaches the Eternal Reality along a particular path: cultural, geographical, biographical. Recently Dom Bede Griffiths, OSB, a Benedictine monk who for the past thirty years has lived in an ashram in India, remarked, 'To me the meeting of Western religions with the religions of the East is really one of the focal points of human development today. I do not feel that religions can go on simply following their own paths separately. We have reached a point in evolution where we have to meet. We have to share, to discover one another.'

This is beginning to happen all over the world, so that a new kind of spirituality is starting to emerge. We are gradually discovering what unites rather than what divides. In 1986 Pope John Paul II invited the leaders of the world religions to join with him in Assisi to pray for world peace. 'I'll wait for you there,' was his simple message. 'Meet me there and we shall pray together.' In the theatre we know that a play only works when all its actors are united in an ensemble. Whether I sit in silence at a Quaker meeting, kneel before the Blessed Sacrament in Westminster Cathedral as I do frequently, celebrate the Eucharist in an Anglican church, or stand for the long liturgy of the Orthodox Church, I know, deep down, beyond all intellectual debate, that I am a member of the Eternal Church, although outwardly a member and ordained minister of one branch – one of many on the same Tree.

If I believe in the fundamental unity of all religions, why be a priest? Part of the answer is that we need guardians of the faith, appointed for that task, with authority to teach, counsel, heal and celebrate the sacraments. A priest is ordained to do all these things, but above all he is ordained to be a burden carrier: as Jesus said, 'For their sakes I make myself whole [sanctify].' In general, society – and all too often the clergy themselves – look upon the task of a priest as being the executant of an office, putting in so many man hours; but no amount of activity or quantity of work will make up for quality. At the end of the day it is not how many sick have been visited, how many people counselled, how many sermons preached, but the quality of those visits, counsellings and preachings. The public rôle of the priest will manifest itself at different times and in different places, but the underground river of prayer, dedication and sacrifice is continuous. And that, necessarily, is unseen by the world at large. There is the Church visible and there is also the Church invisible. Father Henri Nouwen tells of a priest in America who lives alone with his dog, who celebrates Mass daily, and for the rest of the day prays. There is no other outward form of his ministry, and though his bishop has not found it easy to accept, he has nonetheless encouraged him.

There are many gifts and many diversities of rôles, and this is bound to be even more marked in the non-stipendiary ministry, whose members earn their living like other people – and those jobs have to be done well or else their holders will be guilty of trying to serve two masters and failing to serve either. Like other people they know what it is to be unemployed, declared redundant; or be self-employed, knowing, as I did for many years, what it is to be unable to draw the dole and, because of occasional modest royalty payments, being unable even to claim social security. All my life I have been wary of professional clergy who, when people are in distress, offer them the usual counsel, safe within their own professionalism. Only a few have won through, by means of their own suffering and prayer, to a true inner authority.

The non-stipendiary or self-supporting ministry has one task, and the stipendiaried another. There will always be a need, as Bishop Stephen Verney observed in *Towards A New Age*, for a permanent skeletal force to run the great centres and carry on the necessary bureaucratic work of the Church, but alongside this there is also a need for a ministry that can reach out to those places that the 'professional' often cannot. The non-stipendiary priest is able to travel more lightly and, when needed, anonymously.

There are some non-stipendiary clergy who experience, as do many priests today, both Roman and Anglican, a crisis of identity. They often encounter jealousy from their paid-up brethren who look down on them as amateurs. I have even seen non-stipendiaries referred to as 'part-time' priests, which of course is a contradiction in terms. You can be a part-time social worker, plumber or teacher, but you cannot be a part-time priest. A priest is a priest is a priest, *in aeternam*. There can be no crisis of identity if we know who we are and why God has placed us here. Every moment of our lives, *whether others see it or not*, is an exercise of that priesthood. People do not always have to know. Labels are a great problem: stick a label on someone and it is often impossible to see the person underneath. Dog collars are the worst kind of label – which does not mean, however, that they should not be worn.

The characteristic presence of the priest is contemplative; he is there to give witness to what is real. He is not a psychologist, a sociologist, a politician nor an economist. He makes God explicit in his ministry of the Word and the Sacrament: the rest is reserve and silence. The priest is the guardian, the bearer of an order which is greater than his personal vision. It is possible that there is no longer a place in our society for the priest, no rôle other than that of the priestly presence, and yet, at the contemplative level, as he becomes more 'hidden' within our society, the more he may have to contribute. Jonathan Miller, the theatre director and doctor of medicine, observed in a recent lecture for the Squiggle Foundation in London how there are people who are 'neither fish, nor fowl nor good red herring', those who have a quality of not being either this or that: which is to say that they do not have the quality of being people that we recognize. We cannot easily affix a label to them. Such a person he terms an interstitial person: one who stands at the crossroads of society, at a frontier, a place not classifiable. The shaman, the priest, the healer, he maintains, are such people. Their task is to stand at the intersection of paths, between time and eternity, life and death, body and spirit.

One has to be wary of too much argument, with each party trying to prove it is right. If we are to transcend differences then we have to meet one another in love; only then will we experience a oneness with all creation, the Opus Dei. In *Tao te Ching* Lao Tzu said 'Love the world as your own self and then you can truly care for all things', long before the birth of Christianity. That saying, like so many from the *Tao*, prefigures much that is to be found in the teachings of Jesus and points to the common root of all the great spiritual traditions. What is needed today is not argument but prayer, and from prayer grows the tree of love with its ancient roots. As the great Jesuit theologian Teilhard de Chardin puts it, 'It is not a tête-à-tête, or a corps-à-corps, that we need but a heart-to-heart. If the synthesis of the spirit is to be brought about in its entirety (and that is the only possible definition of progress) it can only be done, in the last resort, through the meeting, centre to centre, of human units, such as can only be realized in the universal, mutual love.' In order to reverse a negative and destructive trend in society today we do not need to return to conventional religion so much as turn to a spiritual renewal. What humanity needs today, as Alan Watts* observed, is the means to bring about a widespread shift in consciousness. This will come about through the revival not of any particular religion but of the techniques and experiences that once gave these teachings life and effectiveness.

Many have had to shed their inherited Christianity and rediscover the spiritual by another path. Sally Miles, the actress daughter of Sir Bernard Miles who founded the Mermaid Theatre, is one such person. She had a long struggle with Christianity and could not accept her father's Nonconformist view of life, that we were not put into this world to be happy. When she started practising Buddhism it was, she remarked, 'as if I were looking through a new pair of glasses – everything seemed sharper, clearer, cleaner'. It changed her life in many ways, for she had always had a yearning to develop the spiritual side of her life. Above all, it enabled her to come to terms with a rare degenerative disorder called motor neurone disease – from which the actor David Niven died – which affects the nerve cells linking

*Alan Watts: British born author whose writings on Taoism, Buddhism (especially Zen) were influential in the 1960's especially.

the brain to the muscles, causing loss of movement in the hands, arms and legs and also severely impeding speech and swallowing. It usually results in total physical incapacitation (only the brain remains active) and death within eighteen months to five years: above all, there is no cure. The week in which she had her first fall was the week in which she first heard about Nichiren Shoshu Buddhism, which teaches how one can change one's karma (life tendency) through chanting and daily prayers, and take full responsibility for one's own life and everything that happens to one. At first she saw getting better only in terms of arresting the disease and walking again, but then she came to see it more in terms of making her entity of life stronger. She believes fundamentally in the Buddhist principle of cause and effect – in other words, her life is the way it is now because of things she has said and done, not just in this lifetime but also in past lifetimes.

We all have much to learn from Buddhism about the need to accept responsibility for ourselves, and to realize that many illnesses and problems are the direct result of misuse of one's self, of life, of others; that we also inherit, either genetically or psychologically, certain patterns from our parents and forebears. We have to work at all these problems ourselves, using each moment as an opportunity for redemption in the sense of making whole.

At the first Pentecost, tongues of fire descended and everyone heard the disciples speaking in their own tongue, yet each understood the other. It seems that today, increasingly, the light is breaking through unexpected cracks and apertures, through women and men of varying and often contrasting cultural and religious backgrounds. Christianity is not the sole transmitter of this light. Yet nothing contradicts, because at the centre all speak of the same divine reality, some more purely than others, for much depends upon the discipline and purity of the human vessel through whom these truths are transmitted. 'We are already one,' wrote Thomas Merton. 'But we imagine that we are not. And what we have to recover is the original unity. What we have to be is what we are.'

We must not weep at an end
For there is no end.
We are not what we were.
We cannot lose what we have gained.
We have met, we have touched each other with smiles,
Exchanged unknown emotions.
We have embraced without shame.
We have met for a reason,
A brief interlude in time,
And we part, the purpose done.

David Burrows

4

An Urgent Presence

When I was at Oxford I was often confused as to which direction I was meant to take: whether to be a monk, a writer, a teacher or an actor – I had not then learned about being a director. Now I know that I am all these and there is no conflict. Each of us is many people and, as with any community, it takes time and patience to forge a unity, so that the many selves work in harness, complementing one another. In the theatre I have directed many kinds of plays, not all of which I have enjoyed, but they have been necessary in order to keep alive. In my workshops I have been able to explore at a deeper level, finding the relationship between theatre and ritual. It is rare, however, that one's vocation and avocation became one. Such an opportunity came in 1972 when I was invited by Alexander Schouvaloff, then director of the North West Arts Association, to direct the Chester Mystery Plays for the 1973 Chester Festival of Arts. The plays are presented every five years and are usually spread over two evenings – the Old Testament on one, the New Testament on the next – and then repeated over a period of two weeks. My brief from Schouvaloff was to prepare an adaptation and production that would run not longer than two and a half hours, inclusive of interval, and so could be performed nightly over the fortnight. I was also asked to break with the past style of presentation, which had employed casts of up to two hundred, in medieval costume, and had leaned heavily upon the pageant approach.

Throughout the early stages of preparation I had in mind the original intent of the plays: in an age when most people could not read, they were a means of instructing the faithful in the rudiments of their faith. Our society today, however, is neither wholly Christian nor Catholic, while many in our audience would be members of another religious culture, agnostic or even atheist. How was I to communicate these stories to them? In pondering the problem I was reminded of a remark by Krishnamurti that if only we would read the Bible as great poetry it would yield up a richness of meaning at many levels. Thus the story of the Garden of Eden is a metaphor for a very real human experience as well as being a theological parable. The loss of innocence and the corresponding movement towards new knowledge is something that we all have to live through with varying degrees of pain, experiencing in different ways an 'expulsion from Eden'. The rest of our lives is spent in attempting to rediscover, at a more aware level, this state of innocence, of being at one with the divine reality, the original pattern. Therefore in our staging of this scene at Chester all the women played Eve, and all the men Adam, the many Eves and the many Adams each eating their own apple, while baskets of apples were also handed out to the audience, emphasizing this shared experience deep in the collective unconscious.

It was only after auditioning several hundred people that I finally selected a team of thirty actors who were to treble and quadruple rôles. I then began a series of workshops, with ten actors in each, which were aimed at dissolving barriers, creating an atmosphere of trust and preparing the way for the time when the full company would come together. These sessions enabled me to observe more closely the actors I had chosen, to learn about their potential and to develop exercises related to major themes in the plays. We spent one weekend exploring the Lord's Prayer. Curiously, the Chester Cycle gives nothing of Christ's teaching, and so I had decided to insert into the second half both the Beatitudes and the Lord's Prayer. As Christ spoke the prayer, so the actors would speak it after him, phrase by phrase, each in her or his unique way; not spoken in unison with faultless diction, nor yet rattled through thoughtlessly as it so often is in churches and chapels. In the workshops I invited each person to say the prayer in front of the others. The results were predictable. Only two actors, both older people, made the words well up from within their depths. I then began to probe, questioning and challenging: You say 'Our Father', but why *'Father'*? What picture does that word conjure up for *you*? What impression did your father make on you?' In questioning like this, one has to guard against intellectualizing. It is all too easy to drift into a theological discussion on St Paul's definition of men as no longer slaves but sons of God, and so forth. Then, also, what of women, and God as mother: how do they feel about this? It is not concepts one is in search of, but something felt by the individual, a personal, gut response.

We took the words, 'Who art in Heaven'. *Who art? Thou* art. Yet how can we even begin to comprehend the infinity of God's Being? It cannot be grasped intellectually. So what is in our minds and hearts as we say these words? In this exercise each of the actors found themselves up against their own experience or lack of it. The best touched deep wells within themselves; they all made some discovery. I recall Hywel Jones doing this exercise in the Stage Two Workshop at Hampstead. He began by singing the words 'Our Father' over and over with a deep yearning, accompanied by a cradling movement of the arms. But he got stuck on the words 'Who art'. He could go no further and kept on repeating the words with increasing distress until the immensity of their meaning overwhelmed him and he broke down. He found himself personally, emotionally, confronted with the majesty, the sternness, the *unknownness*, of God. Out of this breakdown there rang out the cry, *'Forgive!'* Quite instinctively, out of his deep personal need, he had jumped to this section of the prayer. 'Forgive us', he continued and then, aware of the link between the words 'us' and 'our', he began to repeat the word 'us' more and more forcefully, hissing the 's' sound so that the word took on the quality of the word 'sin' and finally became that word: 'Sin, sin, sin, sins, sins, sins, sins, forgive *us*, *us*, *us*, forgive *us*, our *sins*!' As a result of this exercise Hywel Jones earned the right to say the Lord's Prayer.

At the end of each of these workshops I invited the actors to say the Lord's Prayer once again, each on their own, one by one. On one occasion there were two individuals who found they could not go on beyond a specific phrase and they stuck there. Their minds went blank. One was the son of a clergyman; he had said the Lord's Prayer since childhood but now he had found an impasse within himself. It is significant that he chose to drop out of the production. One of the actors sighed deeply on the words, 'Give us our daily bread', while another paused long before the final word in 'Deliver us from – evil'. As each of them spoke, so the words were now charged with meaning, with personal associations deeper and richer than any words could express; for it is the *tone* of voice that conveys the truth, something few clergy really appreciate. From the way in which Dorothy Stacey spoke the line, 'Deliver us from evil', we learned more about the nature of evil than from the word itself. Slowly, each member of the cast – in real life farmers, housewifes, teachers, estate agents, travel agents, students, lecturers and nurses – began the process of stripping away the cliché, the sentimental or stock response, learning to stand naked to the words and the experience.

The day that the entire company assembled for the first time was a shock. Suddenly it seemed like a lot of people and yet, even so, all too few for the task that lay ahead of us. I suggested that we should sit in a circle, close our eyes, and then out of the silence speak whatever was our strongest thought, if we had one. Mine was that I felt quite inadequate to the task, not in any negative sense but in terms of a realization of the responsibility. In *The Tempest* Prospero says, 'I have promised to deliver all', and at such a moment the director cannot but feel like Captain Cook leading his sailors on a voyage into the unknown. John Fox, a senior lecturer in drama, commented on the unique experience of these workshops, on how the actors had been able to relax because there had been none of the customary pressure, so familiar in amateur circles, to get the show on. Someone else observed how the improvisations had given her the feeling of belonging to a group, of being totally at ease and able to trust her fellow players, not afraid to reveal the deepest emotions. Over the remaining months we used these Quaker-like silences on a number of occasions, allowing the essential things to rise to the surface. Only after five months were scripts handed out and parts allotted.

Rehearsing a text for the stage can often raise problems never contemplated by the scholar or theologian. One evening I went to visit the Dean of Chester. 'Dean Addleshaw,' I said, 'I have a problem. What did Jesus wear at the Resurrection? The shroud was neatly folded in the tomb, so was he naked or did he have a suit run up by little Jewish tailor? In other words: *what* does the actor wear on stage?'

At that moment all the Dean's clocks began to strike, chime and boom the hour of seven.

'Dear me!' he murmured. 'No one has ever asked me that. I'll have to consult my books. Can you come back in a few days?'

A week later, still without an answer, I went down to Robertsbridge in Sussex to see Malcolm Muggeridge. On arrival I put the same question to him.

'My dear boy!' he beamed. 'He was clothed in *transcendental glory*!'

Alexander Schouvaloff suggested that I stage the plays inside a big top rather than on the Cathedral green as had been done in previous years. My original intention was to present the action on horse-drawn carts, the carts forming various formations, and the audience mobile as in a promenade production. I wanted to use real animals: a lamb for Abraham, a donkey for Baal (which, later, would carry Mary to Bethlehem and Jesus to Jerusalem), horses for Herod's knights, chickens, bantams and sheep for the Nativity scene, and a hundred white doves for Pentecost. The animals were to be in pens around the perimeter of the tent; I wanted the smell and presence of the animals as at a circus. Instead of one adult angel for the Annunciation and similar scenes, I chose a band of scruffy small boys on bicycles, racing from one part of the arena to the next, bearing their messages, ringing their bells boisterously, singing Glorias hoarsely, always a little breathless, and often late. Two of these were to have the special task of following the animals with brush and pan. Quite soon I began to receive letters from the admirable and quite unflappable Festival secretary, Mary Whitehead.

> 'Talking about cows, I have had a conversation with a local established farmer who tells me that to use a cow of any sort in a production is a tall order. First of all, it would have to be a cow that was used to the show-ring and being handled, and it would have to be under constant care during its acting career. Its natural inclination is for food and if it was fed from the hand it would soon get bored after its appetite was fulfilled and would want to wander about. He also says that cows in general are not too hot on hygiene

and would need a full-time attendant (an adult angel) on this point alone. Unless we can find someone who is willing to bring the animal in and out of Chester for each performance, it would have to have a special pen all to its very own self. The days when cows mixed with humans seem to have disappeared. They have become gregarious and prefer company of the four-legged kind.

Pigs are an even worse problem; unless they are infants under six weeks old they are almost impossible to handle and likely to run beserk at the first given opportunity.

Further letters arrived about horses, sheep, and finally pigeons.

I spent quite some time yesterday afternoon talking to Mr Challinor, who is a very experienced pigeon breeder, and his views are as follows:

a. White pigeons are available but only in limited numbers, but it is possible to obtain birds that have a slightly blue cast to them which from a distance would look white. In this way you could make up the hundred you require for Pentecost.

b. The birds would have to be brought to the tent in baskets ready to be opened at the proper moment.

c. Once the basket is opened the birds will fly in an upwards direction, and unless there could be a large opening in the top of the tent, through which they could escape, they will fly round in circles and eventually roost on whatever is available at the top of the tent. Apparently they will remain there for days on end and there are no means of tempting them down. If there is nothing on which they can roost they will then drop to the floor and presumably sit on the audience, which Mr Challinor feels could be more than unpleasant for the people concerned.

d. There is the added problem that the time of the production coincides with the racing season and fewer birds would obviously be available. It was also pointed out that they would not fly in the dark and as you do not intend to use them until the end of the performance they would not return home, even if they could get outside the tent, so therefore there would be the problem of getting them back into their baskets for the next performance.

Mr Challinor did say, however, that he would be prepared to help in every way possible, and if you can think of some way of using the birds, bearing in mind the above points, I will get back to him again. I do hope you have a very happy Christmas and a wonderful 1973.

Yours sincerely,
Mary Whitehead.

I sent to her, and to each of the actors, a Christmas card bearing a design of a white dove holding an olive branch. No animals were used in the production. We did try a donkey, but each time it was urged to the ramp it simply dug in its heels and pulled in the opposite direction.

Instead of a promenade production, therefore, I designed a large circular stage from the centre of which rose a thirty-foot-high pine tree, its branches lopped off to short stumps, but leaving some greenery at the top. This was the Cosmic Tree, the axis between Heaven and Earth, down which Lucifer climbed at the start. Hung with baskets of apples it became the Tree of Knowledge of Good and Evil; it served as a mast for the Ark, and at the end of the first half, when Mary entered the Temple for Simeon to bless the Child, it was hung with evergreen wreaths and storm lanterns, becoming a giant Christmas tree. In the second half it became the cross. At the back of the stage stood rough wooden screens, twelve feet high, with shelves and wooden pegs; here all the props were kept in full view of the audience, which was ranged round in a semi-circle on benches in an auditorium that seated eight hundred people.

Religion is, in essence, symbolic, speaking of a truth beyond finite comprehension, and every religious symbol, when it originated, was an experience surpassing conscious knowledge; such new symbols are manifesting themselves all the time. One of the most valuable of Jung's achievements is to have reopened the way to symbolic thinking, enabling modern man to understand the religious ideas of every race and time, to understand his own religion in a deeper, more vital way, and to find and experience those symbols which come to him from the depths of the unconscious. It is the rôle of the artist to bring to the surface new images and symbols, thereby interpreting and rediscovering ancient truths. Working with the cast of the Chester Mystery Plays over a period of nine months (for the first five in a series of workshops that explored the archetypal themes of the stories) I knew that, when we came to the staging of the Last Supper and the Crucifixion, we had to avoid the over-familiar and conventional representation of these scenes. In such instances one always goes back to the sub-text to ask: What is really happening here?

Over the months we all undertook considerable research. One of the books we studied was *The Ceremonies of Judaism* by Abraham Z. Idelsohn, from which we learned that from oldest times the Jews have celebrated their festivals with special lights. The obligation to kindle these rested on the women. The table was then set for the evening meal and the women attired themselves in Sabbath garments. Before all meals at which bread is served the Jew is obliged to wash his hands and while doing so to pronounce a blessing, because he is to be purified for the table as a priest is for the altar on which sacrifices are made. But Jesus took the traditional Passover meal and charged it with new meaning; and the more I meditated upon the Last Supper as an *agape*, a love feast, in which the body of the beloved is eaten, the more I saw it as a mandala with Christ at the centre, Himself the feast, ringed round by his disciples, and enclosed by a circle of flame like the tongues of fire at Pentecost.

At the beginning of the scene, therefore, the entire company entered singing a chant based upon the single word 'Alleluia'; the women, each with a towel over one arm, carried wooden bowls filled with water. They stood on the perimeter of the circle as the men approached for the washing of hands. The actor playing Christ remained in the centre of the stage, naked to the waist, wearing white cotton trousers. The men lowered over his head a circular cloth with a hole in the middle, until he was standing in the centre of it, while they knelt round him, holding the material taut so that it had the appearance of a round table, with their heads and shoulders appearing above it. While this was happening the women were re-entering with seven-branched candelabra holding lit candles which they set down all round the stage. Taking a flat, circular loaf (baked specially for each performance) Christ blessed and broke it, leaning forward from the centre of the 'table' to give it to the disciples in turn, saying, 'Eat my body'; similarly, after blessing the cup, he passed it round, saying, 'Drink my blood'.

When the meal had ended and Judas had left, the men let go of the cloth and the actor tucked the centre part into his waistband so that it hung from his waist like a robe. I had originally intended that Christ should wash the feet of the eleven, taking as long as might be necessary to do this. The command to wash one

another's feet is strangely ignored by the Church except in a most
token way by religious communities. The deeper significance of
this ritual is worth pondering. However, in the production Christ
washed only Peter's feet, and then the others, following his
example, began to wash each other's feet,

> Since I have washed your feet here,
> I, Lord and Master, in meek manner –
> Do each to each so in fear
> As I have done before.
> Here truly is my bidding,
> Love each other in all thing
> As I have done before.
>
> Chester Mystery Plays

One Saturday I took the men for a special session relating to the
Last Supper. Seating them in a close circle I asked them to focus
on Ian Lever, the young farmer who played Christ, and to be
aware that this was the last meal they would have together. They
were to memorize this moment for all time, rather like Garbo as
Queen Christina when she says, 'I am memorizing this room. In
the future, in my memory, I shall live a great deal in this room.'
The hour, the place, each other's faces, the departure of Judas,
everything that Jesus had said and done, even though they could
not wholly understand it, they were to absorb – knowing that it
was for the last time. And the intensity of this concentration must
communicate itself to the audience. At the end they were to sing a
hymn as the disciples did before leaving for the Garden of
Gethsemane.

For over half an hour they sat in silence and then, very quietly,
they began to sing

> Abide with me, fast falls the eventide,
> The darkness deepens, Lord with me abide!

As they sang on, so the words gathered an intensity of emotion
peculiar to the situation; the disciples looking to Jesus on the
words, 'I need thy presence every passing hour', and he looking
upwards, to his Father, on the words, 'O Thou who changest not,
abide with me'.

> When other helpers fail and comforts flee,
> Help of the helpless, O abide with me . . . .

I need Thy presence every passing hour . . . .
What but Thy grace can foil the tempter's power . . . .
Change and decay in all around I see;
O Thou, who changest not, abide with me!

During the singing of this hymn John Fox, as John, spontaneously reached forward to touch the hand of Jesus. Ian Lever, sensing this, held his hand, while with his other he reached towards David Burrows, as Peter, to take his hand. One by one the actors began to link hands as they knelt in a circle. Slowly Ian Lever lifted them to their feet, raising their hands in the air like a benediction and then, deliberately letting go, breaking the link — for they must learn how to detach themselves from his physical presence. Gently he took John Fox's hand and, placing it in that of David Burrows, sealed up the ring once more, while he stood outside, ready to depart. Out of such improvisations did the entire production grow, scene by scene.

The scene that took much preparation and was possible only because of the months of workshops was the staging of the Passion and the Crucifixion. I had prepared the actors for this by a series of vocal exercises, breaking down the two words, 'Ba-ra-abba-s!' and 'Cr-u-ci-fy!' into their separate syllables. My task was to unleash a ferocity and barbarity of emotion: the word 'barbarity' itself carries an association with the name of Barabbas.

In one of our group discussions we talked about the Crucifixion as an historical event, but then went on to ask: What is crucifixion? Daily we crucify one another: husbands and wives, mothers and children, teachers and pupils, politicians, clergy, civil servants; we are all guilty of cutting each other down to size, castrating one another emotionally and psychologically, dragging people down into the mud. It was this sudden appearance of the word 'mud' that led the way into the scene. The actor playing Christ stood in the centre of the stage, facing Pilate, while the rest of the cast stood upstage, holding long poles with which they began to taunt him, elongating the sounds of 'Barabbas' into a frenzy of hatred and rejection. At the climax of the sound one of the actors began to throw mud at Christ, then more, until suddenly the whole cast were dragging him on the floor around the arena in a cacophony of noise until he was blackened from head to foot and thrust up on the tree, suspended by his arms from two stumps. Then in long, elongated sounds, Ian Lever as Christ cried out, over and over again, 'Eloi! Eloi! Lama sabachthani? [My God, why have you forsaken me?]' Slowly, as they realized what he was saying, the rest of the cast began to climb the tree until they all hung from it like a swarm of bees, taking up with Christ the lament of 'Lama, Lama, sabachthani'.

For what we had learned is that Calvary is both the experience of one person in time and history, and also universal experience: for each one of us, at some moment, has this feeling that God does not exist and that life is without meaning. As a result of this new way of seeing the Crucifixion, avoiding the conventional cross, many non-Christians who subsequently saw the play performed were deeply moved and involved. There were also those Christians who were shocked, while many, especially monks, nuns and priests, wrote to say how they had been affected, shaken and changed by the experience. The intensity of hatred in the cries of 'Barabbas!' and the voice of Christ cutting across this with the long phrases of 'Eloi! Eloi! Lama sabachthani!', his voice spanning octaves and breaking, was something the actors never lost. The whole sequence of lamentation from the cross lasted seven minutes, a very long time in the theatre. Always, of its own volition, it would cease and then, in the silence, would be heard the voice of Christ saying, 'It is finished!'

Alexander Schouvaloff came to see a run-through. 'You'll remember,' he said, 'months ago I explained to you that I wanted this production to break away from the traditional presentation in the manner of a pageant, and, instead, be done in such a way as to be meaningful for today's audience – which would be almost certainly largely not Catholic or even Christian. Well, your production and company succeed in a way which I never imagined or hoped for, by creating something really wonderful which makes sense and will make people think. It is, of course, a production which people will not expect and perhaps one which some will not like. This is what I really wanted. It is also funny. The total balance is there – perfectly. Your production is a rediscovery and your company makes it so. I do not think that professional actors could achieve this degree of commitment.'

In the event the production broke all previous box office

records, and Andrew Porter, who had just returned from reviewing Peter Brook's *Orghast in Persepolis*, wrote in the *Financial Times*,

> This is an exhilarating, exciting and moving experience, and Mr Roose-Evans has come closer to catching the spirit of a communal and contemporary dramatic presentation of matter familiar to all – closer to the spirit of these mystery plays – than one could have thought possible in the twentieth century. The actors played, declaimed, moved freely and fully, without self-consciousness. Ian Lever's strong, unaffected Christ, and David Burrows shining Abraham and Peter were exceptional. The text was largely re-written – but underpinned every so often with a return to that Chester metre of three four-beat lines rhyming, and then a shorter one.

After the final performance David Burrows handed me a poem.

> We must not weep at an end
> For there is no end.
> We are not what we were.
> We cannot lose what we have gained.
> We have met, we have touched each other with smiles,
> Exchanged unknown emotions.
> We have embraced without shame.
> We have met for a reason,
> A brief interlude in time,
> And so we part, the purpose done . . . .

In *The Empty Space* Peter Brook has written, 'The search today is for a necessary theatre, one which is an urgent presence in our lives, speaking to its audience at a depth of feeling that precedes the dissection of man into social and psychological categories, *speaking to a man in his wholeness.*' In that sentence one can replace the word 'theatre' with the word 'art' or the word 'Church'. The search today must be for a necessary art, and a necessary Church, one which is an urgent presence in our lives. If we can but give form to our feelings, define them rhythmically, dramatically, liturgically, tonally; if we can fashion images of what it is we fear, desire, need, hunger for, aspire to; then that form will define the inner turmoil and become detached from us, made objective, ritualized, so that we can begin to meditate upon it and so grow. This process will lead on the one hand to the evolution of new rituals, matching the needs of a vast number of people, all in different situations, cultures and societies, each individual becoming, in a sense, their own Church, both priest and congregation. At the same time it will lead to a deeper, enriched understanding of existing rituals and liturgies. We have to learn how to reinterpret the liturgy and rituals of our particular traditions in the same way that the Bible can be endlessly rediscovered. For the Christian, too, there is a continuing revelation, the Spirit blowing where it chooses. Only in this way can liturgy and ritual became once again dynamic and meaningful realities in our lives.

Ritual goes deep. One cannot play at rituals. A ritual puts one in touch with the elemental and the transcendental, with that which is deep within us and that which is beyond us and which we call God. A pilgrimage is not simply a journey to a sacred place. Although a pilgrim is an ordinary person, he is proceeding through extra-ordinary space, *en route* to his roots. One cannot book a pilgrimage through a travel agency – only the ticket. One goes on a pilgrimage when the call comes and not before. Certain rituals are timeless, shaped, perfected and handed down across the centuries in the form of the great liturgies. Other rituals are created for a specific need, time and space. I would like to quote two examples.

When Karol Wojtyla (the present Pope) became Bishop of Cracow he had a secret fear that his new position would isolate him to some extent from the people, so he began a practice which he continued as long as he remained in Poland, and which was to spread all over the country: *oplatek* parties, something like the *agape* feasts of the West. The *oplatek* is the white wafer of unleavened bread which the Poles traditionally break into pieces on Christmas Eve and share with each other as a sign of love and friendship. It is, as Mary Craig observes in her book *Man From A Far Country*, a kind of secular Eucharist, a symbol of solidarity. He began this practice at the students' church in Cracow and the ritual spread rapidly to other churches, but he wanted to reach out to those who were not believers; he wanted, he said, 'to bring everyone to the white wafer of love.' So each week he would invite groups of doctors, artists, scientists, lawyers, workers and students, whether they were believers or not. They would arrive

at his tiny apartment for a special kind of party. There was no
food, but the table would be decked out as though for a banquet,
and the evening would begin with this simple ritual: a glass of
wine and the sharing of the white *oplatek* wafers. He knew
everyone by their Christian name, and the evenings would often
end with music and singing. He had a special gift for drawing
people together, bringing out what they had in common rather
than what divided them. This simple ritual led to others, as well as
improvised pilgrimages up into the mountains, sometimes in deep
snow.

The second example demonstrates an attempt to unite the
natural and the supernatural, Earth and Heaven, by a small group
of Benedictine nuns at Stanbrook Abbey in Worcestershire,
England. I quote from a letter written in December 1976 by Sister
Meinrad Craighead, OSB:

The winter sky, when dark is uppermost, is a long silent lesson on
the divine order of the heavens. I cherish this relationship between
'gazing' and 'contemplation', and the original meaning of the word
CON-TEMPLATIO i.e. the Roman seers carefully perusing their
specific area of the heavens, discerning the movements and
messages, and advising their clients in relationship to these divine
secrets. So the original 'temple' wasn't a building on earth; it was a
'space' in the heavens. This is exquisite for it implies that the CON
bring the two temples together: they come together when you or I
gaze and *bring* them together. How thrilling that the earth should
reflect that grand order of the heavens: heaven a TEMPLATE for
earth! Oh, this deep, profound winter dance! We are almost
crushed beneath the grandeur of those alive patterns arched over
this tiny sphere.

I lit the Low Solstice Fire late in the evening of the 21st – (o
ORIENS . . .!) and I've such a mountain of debris on the heap that
Brother Fire will burn for days to help the old sun turn the corner
into a New Year. How sweet this Eternal Child who comes out of
the depths of the dark Old Year to bring us the hope and promise of
the New Beginning. Hail Child: King of the Ages! How I love the
long long litany of his Christmas 'names'. I counted them up one
year (from the Advent liturgy) and I believe there were 25 or 30! On
Christmas Day four of us sat at the Fire all afternoon, singing,
chanting, reading poetry, being silent together. Lots of Latin
because most of our Office is in English now so we miss out on the
splendid Latin liturgy. So we take it down to the Fire and weave the

chant into the flames and send the song up as sweet incense. These are glorious days. Perhaps especially so because of the sweet solitude which I was permitted to experience in a hermitage here, which preceded and prepared me for the specific joy of Christmas. There's nothing quite like it, is there? I shall close with this bit from Paul Klee which I love and which seems fitting just now. 'There is something spiritual about the approach of winter. You retire into your innermost chambers and camp near the small glow you find there, the last reserve of warmth, a small part of the eternal fire. A grain of it suffices for a human life.' I hope you have a great roaring fire to heal you and hold your gaze: that beautiful Creature who must tell us so much about the Creator and Creativity. May God our Father give you his Son in full splendour this season, this New Year.

In Christ,
Meinrad.

In subsequent years this small group of nuns would gather round the Solstice Fire on Christmas Eve, sitting beneath the pageant of stars:

I walk, I lift up, I lift up hearts, eyes,
Down all that glory in the heavens to glean our Saviour . . . .
These things, these things were here and but the beholder
Wanting; which two when they once meet,
The heart rears wings bold and bolder
And hurls for him, O half hurls earth for him off under his feet.

Gerard Manley Hopkins

Then from this ritual they would go into the abbey church for the great and solemn liturgy of the Midnight Mass.

Change and experiment in ritual cannot be imposed from the top. It has to start in small groups. At first it may only happen on rare occasions, but slowly it will grow. Naturally there is a danger here. Indeed, whatever we do there are bound to be risks. If we play too safe and stick to the traditions literally, we become trapped in an obsessive observation of detail. But experimentation can lead to eccentricity, over-emotionalism, vulgarization, even to questionable theology, without authority. The quality of what is done, the purity of intention, will depend upon the spiritual and psychological sensitivity and maturity of those taking part; therefore guides are necessary. One of the problems is that all too often it is the clergy themselves who feel threatened, and seek therefore to discourage, repress or obliquely undermine such experiment. One can see this in prayer and house groups. There are clergy capable of merging and being a servant among servants, but all too often they choose to dominate, lead or obstruct. It takes a special kind of wisdom and emotional maturity in any professional to be able to listen to people and to encourage a shared leadership, a shared creativity.

But the rôle of ritual within a religious tradition – Christian, Jewish, Buddist or Hindu – is but one area, and there is need for ritual in a variety of situations outside the church, the temple and the synagogue. And it is here that we need to create safe places – strongholds, refuges, hermitages, retreats, monasteries – places apart, where people can learn to trust one another and themselves, and be able to fashion their own rituals, guided by masters, learning from them and from each other. I am not speaking of jazzed-up services, or folk Masses, in an attempt to popularize church services, nor of cerebral attempts along the lines of 'Wouldn't it be fun if we did so and so'. If new symbols are to arise – and symbols are at the heart of ritual – they cannot be commanded by the intellect. They must well up from within, as they do in dreams. All true art shines through the darkness like the icons in an Orthodox church, illuminated by the votive lamps of the faithful. What is being suggested here is more than self-expression, which is in itself a limited exercise and one that all too often is merely narcissistic. It is rather the discovery of the Self within, the Tao, the God.

When people are given the responsibility of creating their own rituals the result is often surprising. In the summer of 1980 I taught a six-week course on ritual on a campus outside Grand Rapids, Michigan. One of the group, Emily Stuart, a dancer, had to leave halfway through the course in order to return to work in Indiana, and I suggested that the group should create a ritual of farewell. The basic structure was agreed upon by the group in Emily's absence (she being left to create her own contribution), but the detail was left to each individual and not known in advance. On the day itself I acted as Emily's guide. She was blindfolded and led across the campus to where the group were waiting. In my journal I describe it:

Emily is carrying a sack which is enormously heavy. She says it is the burden she wants to carry on this journey and that it

contains her offerings for the group. We come to a path that leads
through the woods, and here Marty has set up a triumphal arch
made of long bamboo poles with newspaper banners streaming
from them. I remove Emily's blindfold and invite her to sit down,
resting her burden, while I bathe her feet. As I do this I speak for
her the poem 'Ithaca' by C. P. Cavafy:

When you set out on your journey to Ithaca,
Then pray that the road is long, full of adventure, full of knowledge . . . .

Always keep Ithaca fixed in your mind.
To arrive there is your ultimate goal.
But do not hurry the voyage at all.
It is better to let it last for long years;
And even to anchor at the isle when you are old,
Rich with all that you have gained on the way,
Not expecting that Ithaca will offer you riches.

Ithaca has given you the beautiful voyage.
Without her you would never have taken the road.
But she has nothing more to give you.
And if you find her poor, Ithaca has not defrauded you.
With the great wisdom you have gained, with so much experience,
You must surely have understood by then what Ithacas mean.

We resume our journey. At a bend in the path we see Marty
waiting in the sunlight (it is a day of heat, blue skies and fleecy
clouds), holding a large, square basket. He is smiling and as he
hands the basket to Emily to put her bundle in, he says, 'Life is a
basket, it will hold your burdens and your joys.' He now
accompanies us, playing his flute.

Further on we see Robin's auburn gold hair in the dappled light
through the leaves. She is weaving a large bouquet of wild flowers
which she places in Emily's basket. 'As you go on your journey,'
she says, 'others will come to join you.'

At the next turn we come across Bill and Kate sitting in the
grass, holding a box of fruit and a container of grape juice which
they place in the basket. Now we come to a choice of paths, and
Bill quotes from a Robert Frost poem:

> Two roads diverged in a yellow wood, and I,
> I took the one less travelled by,
> And that has made all the difference.

The path we have chosen leads now through an open meadow across which comes Dean, leaping up in the air like a jester, waving a scimitar, and signalling us towards Lisa who is seated on a large red and yellow parachute. Here Emily is relieved of her burdens for a while and invited to lie down on the silk, which is then lifted up by the group so that she is carried, gently rocking, as in a hammock or cradle. Finally she steps out of it and it is lifted in the air. She walks beneath it, with a straw hat woven with flowers on her head, and carrying the bouquet, like the Queen of the Feast. Up in a tall oak tree ahead of us sits Roger playing a recorder, and at the foot of the tree a fire is burning. Here we gather for a communal washing of hands, before removing from the fire roast potatoes and corn wrapped in tinfoil. We climb the tree and sit in the tree house or spread out along branches, while Emily now opens her presents – a box of cookies, fruit and an enormous loaf baked by Kim – and these we share in a simple feast. I ponder how we shall end this ritual as they begin to sing, spontaneously adapting for the occasion another Frost poem:

> And I have miles to go before I sleep,
> And miles to go before I sleep.

Emily asks for the Shaker song, 'Simple Gifts', which we all sing with her:

> 'Tis the gift to be simple,
> 'Tis the gift to be free,
> 'Tis the gift to come down
> Where we ought to be.
>
> And when we find ourselves
> In the place just right,
> 'Twill be in the valley
> Of love and delight
>
> To turn, turn,
> Will be our delight,
> Till by turning, turning,
> We come round right.

Looking at her sack, Emily says she has her gifts to offer us but for this she needs to be down on the ground. As we start to climb down we hear shouts from across the field: it is Hywel and Susan coming to join us. The parachute is spread out on the grass in the shade of the tree, and Emily asks us all to sit on it in a circle, with our eyes closed, 'while I prepare my image of what these past three weeks have meant for me'. We hear the sound of water being poured, paper torn, cloth ripped, matches struck – all sounds from our workshops.

'And now,' she announces, 'still keep your eyes closed, but stand up, come a little closer and link hands. Imagine where the centre of the circle is and begin to sing the AH sound. Then, when you feel like it, you may open your eyes and see the image. Eventually you will feel that a part of it is meant for you, and when that happens you should step forward and take it. It is yours. My gift to you.'

We begin to sing the AH sound, the energy coursing through the group, rising and falling, like an onward-flowing stream. When I open my eyes I see in the centre of the parachute, ringed round by our standing figures, a circle of fine pale sand from the river bed and there, placed neatly on it, a smaller circle of twelve beautifully shaped stones and, in the centre of that, one large pear-shaped stone. The image is totally unexpected and moving. The breeze stirs the leaves of the tree and its shadows go flickering across us as the singing grows in intensity, expressing our response to Emily's image. As each feels moved, so in turn we stoop to pick up the stone towards which we feel drawn. Hywel, unsure if there is a stone for him, picks up a handful of the sand. As the singing grows I have a feeling that the stone in the centre is for me and yet I hold back lest this seem egotistical. Then, when all the stones are taken, only one remains, that in the middle, and now I lift it, brush off the loose sand and, kneeling in front of Emily, place it in her hand. She caresses my head. But even as I lift the stone from its bed of sand I am aware that there is something underneath it, half buried, like a small white serpent. Emily now stoops and digs it out, as the group continues singing.

It is a small stone with a hole bored through the centre and threaded through this a loop of cord. She lifts it out and advances towards me. I accept now what is happening and bow my head as she places it over my head and around my neck. I reach out and hold her in my arms and she relaxes, sighing deeply. The singing surrounds us like a waterfall. Then I release my hands and arms, letting her go. Now she moves round the circle, embracing each person in turn, and then at the end walks out of the circle which instantly closes up, so that she is now standing outside, at a distance from the whole experience. She has said farewell and made her exit. The ritual is at end, and we give loud cheers. There is a sudden release of gaiety as we form a cheerful, festive procession, newspaper banners waving in the breeze, flute and recorder playing, and wind our way back through the trees to the studio.

Long afterwards Emily Stuart wrote to me from Indiana about the experience: 'My arms ached for days with the weight of the stones, but I would not have had it otherwise. They were a burden I chose to carry and what I wanted to give, for I had received so much. I am content.'

To speak of an outer journey and an inner journey is perhaps to suggest two separate journeys, as though one were trying to travel parallel paths or changing from path to path. In reality there is only one journey; every journey is also an inner voyage of discovery. Had Emily Stuart not journeyed from Indiana to take part in a summer course she would not have found that very potent mandala which now she carries with her always. As the Zen masters teach us, everything is Tao – the Way.

The creative process, says Jung, consists in the unconscious activation of an archetypal image, and in elaborating and shaping the image into a finished work. By giving the image shape, the artist translates it into the language of the present and so makes it possible for us to find our way back to the deepest springs of life. The true artist, like every gardener, knows how to wait, how to endure, how to suffer: in other words, how to remain vulnerable.

Yet I seriously doubt whether many within the Church understand or appreciate the rôle of the artist. The true artist, and this applies as much to the spiritual process as it does to the creative, goes on growing and is therefore prepared to discard old images of God. Most people, however, do not want to be disturbed. They do not want to acknowledge the awesomeness of God, the pagan or dark side of God. Hence Christianity has become genteel and cosy: the institution takes precedence over the claims, the teachings and the challenge of Christ.

There is a moment in Andrew Harvey's *A Journey to Ladakh* when the Rinpoche, or holy man – one who has achieved perfection – says to him,

> Within this world and within man there are great powers: powers of love, of healing, and of clarity, that can lead a man to liberation. The worse the time – and this present time is Kali Yoga, the Age of Destruction, the more we should look for those powers within ourselves; the more deeply we should strive to obtain them and live them, for our sake and the sake of others. Our terrible time makes the choices clear for us. We will not be able to hide from our responsibilities; we will not be able to pretend that we can go on living without taking thought for our salvation and that of others. We will have to invoke the deepest strengths of our spirit to survive at all.

So what are we to do? The only true way forward is the way within. It is a movement that must well up within each one of us. The way forward is quite simply, and quite drastically, the way inwards, and the 'way in' will then, and only then, reveal the way forward for each one of us.

The ultimate way to God, in all traditions, is through silence, through the hidden martyrdom of prayer. When all words, all thoughts, all feelings, all images are set aside and we rest in the darkness, like a seed in the earth, then He reveals himself to us and we learn our true identity, for He is both the journey and the journey's end.

> To those who have won the victory I will give some of the hidden meaning. I will also give each of them a white stone, on which a real name is written, which no one knows except the one who receives it.
>
> Revelation of St John

The pierced stone which Emily Stuart hid in the sand for me now hangs in my inner sanctum. The invitation to discover our own hidden meaning is extended to all. To each one of us He says

> I am the Way – walk me
> I am the Truth – sing me
> I am the Life – live me

Intermission

You sing, of course you sing, I can hear you;
But make sure that your life sings the same tune as your mouth.
Sing with your voices
Sing with your hearts
Sing with your lips
Sing with your lives.

The singer himself is the song.

ST AUGUSTINE. Sermon 34

ACT TWO: The Map

1

A Journey of the Spirit

If we accept the proposition that man is essentially *homo religiosus* – a religious person – then we have to acknowledge that, unless we recover our capacity for religious awareness, we will not be able to become fully human. The problem, as Laurens van der Post confesses in *Testament to the Bushmen*, is that

> Fewer and fewer of us can find it any more in churches, temples and the religious establishments of our time, much as we long for the churches to renew themselves and once more become, in a contemporary idiom, an instrument of a pentecostal spirit. Many of us would have to testify that, despite the examples of dedicated men devoted to their theological vocations, they have failed to give modern man a living experience of religion such as I and others have found in the desert and the bush.

Whether the Churches can again provide such a living experience of religion (and, of course, many good and holy Christians would claim they can and do), it is clear that in many instances there is a sense of the centre falling apart. Yet this may be only the sign of fundamental change. If Christianity can be truly open in its encounters with the other great religions of the world, and to my mind that is where the real centre of ecumenical activity is to be found, then Christianity may be able to satisfy the surprising hunger for the things of the Spirit that is so often to be found *outside* the churches today. In *A Journey to Ladakh* Andrew Harvey quotes the young Drukchen Rinpoche, and in the following passage I would suggest that the reader substitute for the word 'Buddhist' the word 'Christian'.

A true Buddhist does not remain attached to one tradition or another. He is grateful for what he can learn from the past, but he does not remain addicted to its insights, even to its way of doing things. He is an adventurer and a pragmatist. He does what is necessary at the time it is necessary to do it. Buddhism will change, it must change. It is good if it changes. Change will reveal a new aspect of its truth, a new possibility in its wisdom. Buddhism in the West will be different in many ways from Buddhism as the Tibetan tradition has interpreted it, but why should we mourn that? We should welcome it. No society, no country, no world has a monopoly of spiritual insight, of spiritual truth. At this time of danger, we all, Buddhists, Christians, and atheists alike, should share all the awareness we have, all the compassion we can find in ourselves, and build up every possibility of good will that exists within us towards the world.

The Rinpoche interrupts himself to ask Harvey if he knows the story of the Buddha in the park in the autumn. The Buddha was walking with his disciples through the park covered in autumn leaves when he stopped to pick up a leaf which he held out to the his disciples. 'This one leaf,' he said, 'represents what I have told you. Look at all the other leaves. They are what I have left unsaid.' This story recalls the last verse of St John's Gospel: 'But there are also many other things which Jesus did: were every one of them to be written, I suppose that a world itself could not contain the books that would be written.' The Rinpoche concludes,

> 'Every fresh awareness of Buddhism, every new expression of the Buddhist way, is another leaf. We must be still within ourselves, still and calm, and yet we must also, at the same time, be moving forward, moving further and deeper towards each other, towards the world. What is not useful for this endless transformation must be abandoned; anything that prevents a fine flowering of the spirit must be left behind.'

I have begun with this long quotation from Andrew Harvey's remarkable book because it says so movingly what is already apparent to some within the Church, but which has not yet permeated the whole. Many Christians, perhaps even the majority, feel threatened by any religious tradition other than their own. They cannot acknowledge, let alone perceive, the wisdom and beauty of the Upanishads, the Sufi mystics, the writings of Lao Tzu, the teachings of the Hasid, or of the Buddha, nor see how it is possible to be enriched by these insights and weave them into their own lives as Christians. It is a way, however, that has been pioneered in this century by such individuals as Père de Foucauld, Dom Bede Griffiths, Father Thomas Merton, Teilhard de Chardin, Father Kadowaki, SJ, Dom Déchanet, Dom Aelred Graham, William Johnston, SJ, Father Monchanin, Father Henri le Saux (better known as Abhishiktananda) and many more. As Ursula King has commented in her study of Teilhard de Chardin, *Towards a New Mysticism*, the emergence of a global society has brought with it the idea that we must develop a new consciousness and identity as world citizens, so that 'we perhaps need a new kind of world believer who can meaningfully relate to the perspective of more than one religious tradition, and thereby find a deep enrichment'.

Each of the individuals above (the majority are Roman Catholic) is among the pioneers of such a new spirituality, and represents a genuinely open religious quest, cutting across major religious and denominational differences. On 10 December 1968, the last day of his earthly existence, Thomas Merton spoke these words,

> I believe that by openness to Buddhism, to Hinduism, and to these great Asiatic traditions, we stand a wonderful chance of learning more about the potentiality of our own traditions, because they have gone, from the natural point of view, so much deeper into this than we have. The combination of the natural techniques and the graces and the other things that have been manifested in Asia, and the Christian liberty of the Gospel, should bring us all at last to that full and transcendent liberty which is beyond mere cultural differences and mere externals – and mere this or that.

It was at the first Summit Conference in Calcutta of abbots of Catholic monastic orders and representatives of Asian religions that Merton, leading them in prayer, asked everyone to form a circle and join hands. 'We are going to have to create a new language of prayer,' he said, 'and this new language of prayer has to come out of something which transcends all our traditions, and comes out of the immediacy of love.'

Increasingly the emphasis is upon spirituality rather than upon creeds, rituals or institutions; upon a spirituality that is seen not as an alternative lifestyle nor an escape from Western society, but one rooted firmly in reality, balancing action and contemplation. Fundamentally the search is one for a deeper fulfilment of life; not for *well-being* but rather, as Teilhard de Chardin expresses it, for *more-being*. 'The *homo religiosus* thirsts for the real,' observed Mircea Eliade in his journal, 'he wants to *be* fully at any cost.'

Throughout the ages women and men have been intuitively aware of an inner centre, of a Self beyond the self. The Greeks called it man's inner daemon; in Egypt they spoke of it as the Ba-soul; the Romans referred to it as the genius native to every human being. Quakers speak of it as the inner light which is available to all who learn how to centre down within themselves; while Carl Jung referred to it as the Self, meaning the essential true identity at the heart of each human being, as opposed to the petty tyrant of the ego or self, with a small 's'. Increasingly today people are discovering once again that it is from within themselves that they must find the answer to their own eternal identity if they are to realize and achieve an ultimate meaningfulness in their lives. All who begin to listen to the voice within learn that they have entered upon a religious quest, a journey of the spirit, in search of answers to those ancient questions: Who am I? Where have I come from? Where am I going? They are questions that cannot be answered intellectually but have to be lived, suffered and endured.

The hero in each one of us, once he has set forth on this quest, must undergo many trials before he wins the Golden Fleece, the elixir of life, the crock of gold. Theodotus, writing in AD 140–60, described a gnostic – a seeker after hidden truth – as one who has come to understand who he is, what he has become, where he is, whither he is going, whence he has come, from what he has been released, what birth is and what rebirth. Outside the Church there are countless numbers seeking the answers to these questions, for modern man is indeed in search of a soul. Many discover the first answers through analysis and the intimation and wisdom of dreams; others through encounter groups or other forms of therapy; some through a natural form of meditation. The first step in the quest calls for a commitment and, above all, a discipline on the part of the seeker. The path is different for each individual, yet the end of the journey is the same. Ultimately the discovery of the interior, of the reality within, leads to the encounter with God, so that a natural form of meditation leads on to a supernatural form of meditation. 'The real place of the Divine encounter,' writes Abhishiktananda, 'is in the very centre of our being.' The name of this ultimate encounter is prayer; but for most Christians, and most people, the word prayer has come to be associated with intercessions, petitions and lengthy prayers, or else reflective (meditative in that sense of the word) exercises upon the key episodes in the life of Christ, as in the Rosary or the Ignatian exercises. For those who are drawn to the life of inner prayer I have chosen to use the word 'meditation', implying either the use of a mantra – the repetition of a sacred name – or a practice centred upon breathing which aims, similarly, at emptying the mind of all discursive thoughts and feelings. The aim is to empty and be emptied, so that the soul may be filled with God: breathing God in and breathing Him out.

Many people in search of God are driven away from our churches by the barrage of words employed either in the various liturgies, or improvised in endless prayers and sermons. Prayer, as T. S. Eliot reminds us in *The Four Quartets*, 'is more than an order of words, the conscious occupation of the praying mind, or the sound of the voice praying'. In his book *The Shape of the Liturgy*, Father Gelineau observes, 'We are bombarded with a continual barrage of information, admonitions, and introductions, readings, prayers, prayer intentions, sermon, and the long monologue of the Eucharistic prayer.' In most churches there is also the problem that the readings and prayers are almost always too fast. We forget that the listening ear assimilates more slowly than the reading eye. In addition, few clergy or laity are trained in the use of the voice as an expressive instrument, so that the liturgy of the Word often becomes unintelligible, artificial, theatrical or boring. The overall result is an abundance of words, many of which are inaudible even with the aid of microphones. Amplification has actually made many much lazier about their speech. 'How,' asks Father Gelineau, 'to make space for the heart and the spirit?' How to make space, as do the Quakers, for silence? Indeed, it may be asked, to what extent do our rituals, our liturgies, reflect an interior reality? Though the Mass and the

Eucharist are valid, however they are celebrated, we do need to ponder the way in which our liturgies are celebrated. 'In the hands of the great ceremonialists,' writes P. D. Mehta in *The Heart of Religion*,

> these rituals produced profound psychological effects. *Trained to meditate,* the attention of the skilled celebrant was wholly concentrated upon the psycho-spiritual significance of the ritual. It was the power of concentrated thought of the celebrant and of the devout feelings of the participants which made the atmosphere of the ceremony, exerted the influence for uplift and inner vision in the congregation, and made the ritual a veritable sacrament, a ceremonial magic. The actual presence and benediction of the invoked and worshipped deity was deeply felt. Such magic was essentially a communion with the divine and with nature. The esteem in which the efficacy of the sacrificial ritual was held was expressed in superlative terms by some of the greatest Upanishadic teachers.

It is not surprising that so many of those who are in search of truth turn away from our churches. It is not that we do not require words: all religious traditions have their sacred scriptures, the revealed teachings, but words require space just as a plant needs light. There is a time for speaking and a time for not speaking; a time for words and a time for silence.

I recall reading *The Book of Books* by Idries Shah. I had already bought a number of books on the Sufis and so, seeing this thick, hard-backed volume in the local bookshop, I added it to my collection. It tells the story of a wise man who taught his disciples from a seemingly inexhaustible store of wisdom. He attributed all his knowledge to a thick book which was kept in a place of honour in his room, and which he would allow no one to open. After his death the book was handed down from one generation to another. It came to be known as the Book of Books. On page 11 of Idries Shah's book he tells us the story to this point and then remarks that in the pages that follow we will find the contents of the Book of Books. There follow 260 pages of thick, white and entirely blank paper. Each of those pages I 'read' slowly. I know enough of Sufi teaching jokes to be aware that they are meant to be taken seriously. The reading of those blank pages remains for me still a rich and instructive exercise. I could have cheated, whipped through the rest of the book and said, 'Ah, yes, I get the point!' but that would have been to intellectualize and, therefore, trivialize the experience. At the end, on the final page, I wrote these words, taken from an early Buddhist text, 'The truth was never preached by the Buddha, seeing that you have to realise it within yourself.' Or, as Jesus said, the Kingdom of Heaven is within you.

'Our real journey in life is interior,' wrote Thomas Merton as he was setting off on his last journey to the East, three months before his death. 'It is a matter of growth, deepening, and of an ever greater surrender to the creative action of love and grace in our hearts. Never was it more necessary for us to respond to that action. I pray that we may all do so.' Today so many hunger for the things of the spirit, for the life of grace, and yet all too often they do not find it within our churches. And yet it *is* there, that treasure beyond all price, waiting to be rediscovered, as Teilhard de Chardin found:

> And so, for the first time in my life perhaps – although I was supposed to meditate everyday! – I took the lamp and leaving the zone of everyday preoccupations and relationships where everything seems clear, I went down into my inmost self, to the deep abyss whence I felt that my power of action emanates. But as I moved further and further away from the conventional uncertainties by which social life is superficially illuminated I became aware that I was losing contact with myself. At each step of the descent a new person was disclosed within me of whose name I was no longer sure, and who no longer obeyed me. And when I had to stop my exploration because the path faded from beneath my steps, I found a bottomless abyss at my feet, and out of it came – arising I know not where – the current which I dare to call *my* life.

Similarly in his journal, *Markings*, the late Secretary-General of the United Nations, Dag Hammarskjold, wrote, 'Now. When I have overcome my fears – of others, of myself, of the underlying darkness – at the frontier of the unheard-of. Here ends the known. But from a source beyond it, something fills my being with its possibilities – at the frontier.'

Many, understandably, are frightened of 'losing contact with themselves' as Teilhard de Chardin describes. Many do not want to encounter a new person within themselves; yet this is what

Jesus requests of all who wish to follow him: except a man lose his life he shall not find it. But there is no need to be frightened, for in the life of silent prayer God Himself is leading us, and He will not lead us out of our depth.

The invitation from all the great masters of meditation is always the same: Come and see! But in spite of the many books making such claims there is no easy path. In addition, our Western culture lacks a teaching tradition. To whom can we turn for counsel? There are few masters, and of those who write books on or about meditation (including this one), how are we to distinguish the true from the misguided and, therefore, misleading? The books themselves may recommend different techniques, some of them extremely complicated and esoteric, often alien to a Western culture. It can be very perplexing.

Unless it is our good fortune to meet a true master (male or female) we shall have to persevere alone and, in spite of all mistakes and difficulties, the desire and pursuit of the Whole will bring us a long way; while, ultimately, the greatest of all teachers is God. For the Christian it may be through the person of Christ or, as for Philip Toynbee, of the Holy Spirit, that guidance will come. Often it comes from the most unexpected direction for life itself is our teacher and each incident, obstacle, encounter with another person or animal or nature, may be, for that moment, our teacher. Sadly, and all too often, we do not recognize this until too late. On their way to Emmaus the disciples fell in with a stranger and began to discuss with him those matters that were of urgent importance. As they neared their destination they could have said goodbye to the stranger, but something about the encounter had stirred them and they invited him in. And so it was that they recognized their master and teacher. If we truly seek we shall find the teacher, but first we have to commit ourselves and follow a discipline. Then, when we are ready, the teacher will appear.

If we do set out on the Journey to the East we shall assuredly meet others on the way and in the Way, who will encourage, correct or assist us. Of that there is no doubt. We shall discover that we are in a company of others who are travelling the same path here and now and, more than that, we shall find that we are in a great company of travellers stretching across the centuries

and beyond time. We shall know, from experience, the living
presences of those whose earthly existence has ended but who are
permitted to stand about us, out of time and in eternity.

> They are here now, those who have care of me.
> Their love is like an ocean flowing in
> To enclose an island. Every inlet yields
> To its warm presence. I think that I shall go under
> Like coral in the azure of smooth seas,
> And take my life from such a depth of calm
> I shall become as they are. There is no way
> Outward and upward in this noon of Om
> But this. Beckoned and buoyed by love, I go.
> The place I go to I will build for you.
> You hear me? I must leave now. It is now.
>
> *The Ungainsayable Presence*

Once, arising out of a wordless, imageless meditation, as I
opened my eyes, there came the words, 'God is an endless
journey', words which John Rowlands Pritchard, the calligraphic
artist, subsequently made into an icon for me. This book is a
signpost pointing a way forward on that journey of the spirit,
notes dispatched from the interior by one who is still only in the
foothills. It is a book written *en route* by one who may never
arrive. Yet, as the *Bhagavad Gita* says, 'Even he who merely
yearns for Yoga goes beyond the world of books.' Having once
heard the call, it is enough to set out on the journey. Whether one
meditates well or ill is not really the point. It is enough to
meditate. It is to encourage others in a similar spirit that this book
is written, that they may know that it is possible to arrive at a
stillness and serenity even in the thick of battle.

2

Posture

Though there are many techniques of meditation there is one prime requisite, and that is a proper posture. The true relationship of body, mind and spirit is something which we – especially the pew-oriented Christians of the West – are still slow to understand. In Japan, however, it lies at the centre of the ancient teaching of Hara (the Japanese word for the Vital Centre in man), while in India the practice of Yoga, and in China that of Tai Chi, have pursued a similar path. Japanese who practice Hara rest upright and composed, their whole being gathered inward. Such a person cannot be thrown off-balance as in the many illustrations of the Boddhi-dharma who brought Zen Buddhism to China, and whose image is still given to children in the form of a tumbler doll with a round, lead-weighted belly which always brings him back to his upright position no matter how often he is knocked down.

Those who practise Hara have a right balance with themselves and with others, with animals and even objects. I recall a story told to me once by my teacher, Franz Elkisch. One of his patients was a nun who was restless within herself, and the despair of her community. Nothing that she did ever came right; she was at sixes and sevens with herself and others, always breaking things and having accidents. Through her analysis she began to practise Yoga in the privacy of her cell and to rediscover the relationship between her body, mind and spirit. No one in the community knew this apart from her Abbess. Then, one day, the community's sewing machine broke down and no one was able to repair it. Suddenly this nun 'knew' that she could repair it. The others all laughed and ridiculed her, saying she would only make it worse. She persisted, however, and succeeded in repairing it. From then onwards, instead of things coming apart in her hands, they came together, and the community began to see her in a new light. Her whole relationship with herself and with the community changed.

Our physical posture reveals our inward posture. We have only to look around us to notice the awkward, uncoordinated movement of most people in so-called repose. We see the rounded shoulders of one, the over-emphatic movement of another; here the head jerked back and the chin stuck out; there one shoulder higher than the other; and the many other manifestations of what F. Mathias Alexander* described as bad usage of the self, acquired through bad habits over the years, leading in due course to slipped discs, backache, fatigue, migraine, depression and other problems.

Yet none of this is necessary. Professor Frank Pierce Jones, at Tuft University Institue for Psychological Research, observed how the seemingly effortless and tireless energy of small children of two to three years of age stems from the fact that they have a proper relationship between the head, neck and back, so that they enjoy a perfect balance throughout their whole body, with the result that every action is performed with a minimum of strain and tension. When, however, this relationship is interfered with, the balance is destroyed, so that strain and compensating tensions are multiplied. For example, when a small child stoops to pick up something he moves down smoothly, with the weight of the body in equilibrium throughout the movement and capable of being reversed at any moment without a jerk. An adult performing the same movement loses equilibrium at the start and preserves his balance only by increasing tension, often to such a degree that he has to pull himself up on his toes to stop falling over.

The main problem in re-educating people in the correct use of themselves is, as F. Mathias Alexander pointed out, that we all

---

*F. Mathias Alexander, an Australian, who invented the Alexander Technique, a radical system of body dynamics, a revolutionary and far-reaching method for maintaining the health and efficiency of the body. He taught for many years in England and America, quickly attracting support from leading figures in the arts and the sciences. Famous students such as George Bernard Shaw, Aldous Huxley, and John Dewey, all testified to the dramatic benefits they received from the Technique.

become so accustomed to our usual way of doing things that it feels right to us, so that any more efficient way of doing things is bound, at first, to 'feel wrong'. In addition, the Alexander Technique can be imparted only through the experience of working with a teacher on a one-to-one basis (and not, as is often found in America, working in groups of sometimes as many as a hundred people!). The Technique is not a matter of doing certain exercises nor of osteopathic manipulation, and although one of its effects is to lengthen and strengthen the spine (often adding a quarter to half an inch to a person's height), it has nothing to do with sitting erect like Queen Mary or keeping one's head up. Rather it is a matter of our whole bearing, so that we aquire absolute control over whatever we are doing – whether it is gardening, driving, typing, playing golf or wielding a dentist's drill. To the extent to which we learn not to intrude old habits, and to submit to the manual guidance of the teacher, receiving a new sensory experience, so we find the neck freeing itself, the head and spine realigning themselves and the torso lengthening. The major results of this re-education in what Aldous Huxley described as one of the non-verbal humanities is an overall flexibility of the body, ease of movement, less tension in the jaw and neck, more relaxation in the tongue and throat, and deeper breathing because of the new alignment of the diaphragm. A sense of weightlessness is also experienced, and less effort is required to move one's limbs.

The following passage from P. D. Mehta's *The Heart of Religion* shows how all this applies to the practice of meditation:

> Meditation begins with establishing a calm state. Let the body be at ease, free of all strains in the pelvic and abdominal regions and in the muscles of the shoulders and arms, and especially in the neck which is the connecting link between the head (which contains the brain and all the sense organs) and the rest of the body. Let the back be erect, elastic; imagine the spine is like a spring. Let the head balance finely on the neck and let the muscles around the eyes and lower jaw be quite relaxed. This is essential for establishing my own gentle breath rhythm which will then effortlessly maintain itself without needing special attention. Let elastic ease pervade the entire body. It is the happy peaceful state, essential for meditation.

Without a true understanding of the body, as also of the psyche, the pilgrim on the journey of the spirit is going to be weighted down, quite literally, by much unnecessary baggage. Only when the body is at ease is the mind at ease; only when the mind is at ease is the body at ease. The two go hand in hand.

The Alexander Technique, however, is only one of a number of psycho-physical techniques which include Shinto-Shiatsu and Tai Chi; with such a variety of approaches one marvels at the richness, the manifold nature, of the spirit. Aldous Huxley once described the great flaw in the mentality of Western man as the separation and disassociation of mind and body. Christian mystics especially have tended to neglect the physical side, unlike the contemplatives of the East. In the annual F. M. Alexander Lecture, delivered at the Medical Society of London in 1972, Father Geoffrey Curtis developed this further: 'The extraordinary importance of Alexander's discovery with regard to the effects of a right relationship between head, neck and spine on the whole human organism is itself reflected in the mystical tradition by its unbroken insistence on the spiritual importance of uprightness. It is only the Western mystics who have largely neglected the importance of posture.' He draws attention to the teachings of St Gregory of Palamas and the monks of Mount Athos, who have always insisted that physical deportment is a factor of salient importance in the cultivation of the spiritual life. St Gregory also laid emphasis on the importance of being conscious of the navel and the region below it as of central importance in the spiritual life. This idea is echoed in the teachings of Hara.

Christians have much to learn from the Alexander Technique, the teachings of Hara and the principle of the chakras in Hindu spiritual practice. Indian tradition has always visualized the human body as growing like a plant from the 'ground of the Beyond', the Supreme Brahman, and just as the vital juices of a plant are carried up and outward from the roots through channels and veins, so are the creative energies in the body. The root of the human plant, however, is not below but above – beyond the top of the skull, over the spine; it is through this chakra that the essential and divine energies flow in from the Beyond. After spreading along the body channels they flow to the outermost tips of the senses and even further, out into the space surrounding the physical body, which is referred to as the 'subtle

body'. More than thirty years ago, long before I knew any of the
teachings of other religious cultures, I painted a self-portrait.
That painting was my first intimation of the body as a source of
illumination entering in at many levels. The subsequent experience, years later, of the Alexander Technique, of Shiatsu and
of healing, has deepened this insight. There is another insight here
too: that a simple, primitive self-portrait can be in itself a subject
for meditation, for instruction, drawing us into the interior so
that in due season we may emerge cleansed, baptised, integrated.

   A knowledge of the body and of body language can also be an
aid in distinguishing a true teacher from a novice. I recall going to
learn Insight Meditation from a young English Buddhist monk.
As he stood talking to the assembled group he was constantly
tugging at his robe as repeatedly it slid down and off his shoulder.
This neurotic gesture at once alerted me. Similarly, attending a
workshop on Tibetan chant I observed that the teacher was
physically very restless. Many Westerners today acquire techniques from a year abroad – often taught to them free of charge –
and then return to teach them without being spiritually grounded
in the discipline. The world is full of teachers offering a variety of
expensive techniques, or crowding so many into a workshop that
they make nonsense of group dynamics, albeit often netting for
themselves £2000 in one weekend. The true teacher of any
spiritual discipline will be in themselves a centred person, while
their physical strength and calm will proclaim the strength and
calm within. Such a person is a whole person, in whom each
gesture becomes, quite natually, meaningful, as Andrew Harvey
describes in A Journey to Ladakh,

   The Rinpoche walked slowly. He touched everyone he could,
   sharing himself with all those who asked something of him, advice
   or healing or blessing. He never seemed hurried. Sometimes, when
   he was moving in light, he looked so frail that he was almost
   transparent; at other times he looked as if nothing could tire or
   weaken him. He did not only welcome his own people; to as many
   of the foreigners there as he could he extended a hand or a smile.
   His walking there, his presence, gathered everyone together, united
   everyone and everything in that afternoon, the birds, the flowers,
   the wall, Ladakhi, and foreigner alike.

For the Westerner who meditates there is no reason why she or

he should not sit cross-legged on the floor, even in the lotus
position, provided that the effort of doing so does not distract
from the meditation. Beginners who wish to sit cross-legged are
advised to do some simple Yoga exercise daily until the body finds
such a position natural; it is important to make haste slowly.
However, it is perfectly adequate to sit on a chair, spine erect, the
legs slightly apart and feet resting firmly and squarely on the
ground. Alternatively you can use a low bench a few inches high,
underneath which you can tuck your feet, with your buttocks
resting on the bench. The height of the prayer bench (which can
even have adjustable flaps so that it can be folded flat for travel) is
a matter of experiment. Once you are seated or kneeling, your
hands may rest on your knees or be lightly clasped. Again, there is
no necessity to place your hands in a particular mudra (position)
unless you choose to do so. The important thing – the essential
thing – is to sit with spine erect yet without undue tension or
rigidity. We should not lean or slump. 'The most important
thing,' says Shunryu Suzuki in *Zen Mind, Beginner's Mind*, 'is to
own your own physical body. If you slump you will lose yourself.
Your mind will be wandering about somewhere else; you will not
be in your body.'

However, to sit erect and lightly like this, even for five minutes,
is not easy for most people. The effort to concentrate tenses the
back and neck muscles so that we are continually distracted. In
part this is due to the ego resisting, through the body, our
attempts to still the mind. The body, arch-pretender that it is, puts
on all kinds of acts, feigning physical and mental illness, minor
and major aches and pains, in an attempt to hinder our progress.
The ego knows that it is in the process of being deposed and will
use every trick in its capacious bag to thwart this aim. The
practice of meditation aims at stilling the mind, bringing mind,
body and spirit into one harmony so that in the stillness and
silence we may hear the eternal sound of OM – the voice of God.
Those who practice the Alexander Technique, Tai Chi, Yoga or
Shiatsu, however, will find that they are less likely to experience
this muscular tension; indeed, such techniques remove many of
the initial obstacles experienced by the person learning to
meditate. The ego, needless to say, will find other ways of
attempting to undermine the fragile citadel.

The image of the seated Buddha which dominates much of the religious practice of the East speaks to us of the importance of 'sitting meditation'. 'The exercise of sitting', writes the philosopher and psychotherapist Karlfried Durkheim

> is the most fundamental of all. Here the practice of stillness has its source. A thousand secrets are hidden in simply sitting still. A person who has once learned to collect himself completely in his sitting will never again let a day pass without practising for at least half an hour, for it is this which gives complete inner renewal, especially when he has learned to concentrate exclusively on the sitting, emptied of all thoughts and images.

Master Eckhart, the Christian mystic, was once asked, 'Who made thee holy, brother?' and he answered, 'Sitting still, and my lofty thoughts, and my union with God.'

3

Breathing

If we in the West think about breathing it is as an exercise of the body, and none of us – not even Christians who speak of the Pneuma, the life-giving breath of God – perceives its spiritual potential. In physical training we are likely to be taught to breathe in vigorously, swelling the chest, but we find it less easy to exhale, to let go, and try instead to hold onto the breath. It is as though we had a deep-rooted fear of letting go. It is most noticeable in a crisis when suddenly someone breaks down and lets go: then the breath is shaken out in great sobs as the tension is released. So, strange as it may seem, if we wish to learn to meditate we must first learn how to breathe. It is only when we are able to breathe in and out in a smooth unbroken rhythm, breathing with the entire Cosmos, that we begin to understand the Zen saying that it is not 'I' who breathe but 'It' which breathes me. This sensation that 'It' breathes me is one of the most blissful experiences in the early stages of meditation, a sign of letting go, and the first hint of the ego-lessness of prayer. However, we must learn to let go even of this, for if we hang onto this or any other sensation, then we shall remain trapped in the ego.

In learning to meditate you need to spend quite a lot of time simply breathing in and out in a conscious manner; and the more agitated, worried or distracted you are when you settle down to meditate, the more necessary it will be to spend some time relaxing into the breathing before starting to meditate. Seated erect on a chair, or kneeling on a meditation stool, first allow the stomach to relax and then slowly to inflate, becoming full-bellied as you breathe in. It is important to breathe in from the very root of the diaphragm – but only the diaphragm moves; the rest of the body remains still. After inhaling, gently deflate the diaphragm so that the air is pushed out. And so you continue. The belly inflates and it deflates. The breath flows in and it flows out.

Another way is to imagine the breath travelling the length of the spine until it reaches the top of the skull, and then pause for a moment before breathing out. As you breathe out imagine the breath flowing over your forehead and face, over the chest and arms, down to the genitalia and back to the base of the spine. In this way the breathing becomes a circular motion. As you breathe out it can help to imagine the breath as a waterfall cascading down you. This exercise, which is a Shinto one, can be developed by standing, and imagining the breath flowing up from under the ground into the soles of the feet, up along the backs of the calves, the thighs, on up the spine to the top of the skull and the chakra there, pausing, and then on the release of the breath allowing it to pour down over the face, chest and both legs back into the ground. The third way of doing this exercise is to repeat the one just described but now to imagine that the breath, as it flows up from under the ground, is at a distance of two or three inches from the body. It hovers over the head and flows back into the ground in exactly the same way, but at this slight distance from the physical body. It is rather like putting a shield or veil of protection about us, protecting ourselves from harm. What is valuable about these three exercises, each of which should be done about ten times, is that they generate a great sense of calm. Needless to say they can be done lying down, and my Shiatsu teacher used to teach them to women in a cancer ward in London who were lying tense with anxiety. She enabled them to see how they could help themselves; many a chaplain could learn something from this.

Until your body is calm and centred, you cannot expect to begin meditating. You should think of these exercises as a preparation, although in time they will come to be part of the meditation itself. As you become practised in breathing you can learn to give more thought to a pause on the completion of the indrawn breath, and another after you have exhaled. To do this we breathe in until the breath is completed and then pause, leaning gently on the fullness of the breath as if resting on a wave

that is about to break. Then, as it breaks, we go with it, until the
wave has exhausted itself and we are emptied of breath; then, in
that moment of no breath, we pause, without fear. We dare to let
go utterly, to be emptied. This moment is like a tiny death, but we
are not afraid. A few seconds later, like a wave of the sea, the
breath comes flowing back into our lungs and diaphragm. Like
vessels we allow ourselves to be emptied. The Spirit enters and the
Spirit departs, but always the Spirit returns. We breathe God in,
and we release him to the world.

The breathing must be done very gently. A common difficulty is
that people try too hard – what F. Mathias Alexander referred to
as 'end-gaining'. We are so impatient to see results, but in
meditation we have to learn how to step aside. Most of our
problems in life, as in meditation, stem from the fact that we are
standing in our own light. I once came across some words by a
famous singing teacher which are very relevant here. In his book
Della Voce Umana Vincenzo Vanninni wrote,

> Nature's means are essentially simple; it is only we who complicate
> matters with our pretentious attempts to be helpful. All that the
> singer can do is to remain a spectator. He must cease to interfere
> and, rather, cultivate an attitude of intelligent laziness. Nature has
> no need of assistance. Leave the diaphragm to do its own work;
> neither help nor hinder it, but *leave it alone*. There is no need of
> special methods of breath control for singing, nor is there any lack
> of breath in the normal healthy human being.

After a while our breathing will take care of itself. Sometimes it
may slow down almost to a standstill. You may have read that in
certain advanced meditation states breathing sometimes stops
altogether for a time, but don't try to slow down your own
breathing or even cease breathing. There are advanced techniques
in meditation related to breathing, as there are in Yoga and other
disciplines, but these should not be attempted unless we are in the
hands of a true master over a long period of time – and in the right
climate. In *Ordeal by Labyrinth*, Mircea Eliade observes: 'You
see, it was important to be guided by someone who was both a
doctor and also familiar with the practice of Yoga from personal
experience.'

This breathing is not in itself meditation. It is, at this stage, a
preparation for meditation, just as in a Quaker meeting for

worship the first quarter of an hour, or however long is needed, is there to allow the meeting to 'gather itself' and 'centre down.' After taking up a meditation position and before the breathing exercises, Christians may choose to commend themselves to God the Father (or Mother), God the Son and God the Holy Spirit, making a slow, meditative sign of the cross. The sign of the cross not only invokes the threefold power of the deity in the Christian revelation, but it is also a symbol of the union of all opposites, reaching up into the heights, plunging into the depths, and extending from one side of the universe to the other in an embrace of love. It unites us with all nature and supernature.

Then, thinking no thoughts, we simply observe the breath as it comes in and goes out. Gradually the body is calmed, the mind stilled. It is now that we begin to direct our attention towards an imagined cavity at the centre of our being, where the heart is – and yet that is not the physical heart. Seated upright or cross-legged, or kneeling erect, the hands loosely together or resting on our knees, we concentrate upon this space. It is as though, deep within us at the level of the heart, a lamp is burning, and it is our task to tend this light, to see that it does not go out. We concentrate with mind and heart, body and spirit. Mircea Eliade has pointed out that in the *Upanishads* we find the idea that God (the Spirit) is buried in us as in a cave; he is not dead, but only hidden in there somewhere. The heart, which is where the *Upanishads* locate the presence of the Atman, (the supreme Being) is a 'cave'. The soul is like a treasure, hidden in the midst of the body as in a mountain. Similar images are also found, such as a book hidden for a long time in a cave and rediscovered by chance; or God hiding himself in a pearl that is difficult to find; and in the Mithraic mysteries which were celebrated in real or imagined caves.

For some the breathing-in-and-out may be the meditation to which they are called, and whether they are Christians or non-Christians this practice will lead them to the very heart of the encounter with the divine. In following the meditation of the breath Christians need not fear that they will grow away from Christ. It is important to stress this because many Christians, including professional religious, are frightened of letting go, of possibly losing their preconceived idea of God, and fear becoming possessed by what they think of as 'the devil'. By allowing the Spirit to breathe through us we will discover that Christ is being more deeply centred in us, as we are grounded in the presence and the love of the Father of All Light. We will experience as a living reality that He is in the Father and the Father is in Him, and that Father, Son and Spirit are in us, and in Him we shall become one. We shall also become conscious of the mysterious presence of Sophia, the Eternal Wisdom, the Feminine Principle: 'Listen to me, then, you that are my sons, that follow to your happiness in the paths I show you; listen to the teaching that will make you wise, instead of turning away from it. Blessed are they who listen to me, keep vigil, day by day, at my threshold, watching till I open my doors. The man who wins me, wins life, drinks deep of the Lord's favour.'

Others, however, will be drawn to the use of a mantra – a sacred word or phrase – as the basis of their meditation, so that in them the Word is made flesh, quite literally. Even here, however, the breathing will provide the essential foundation for a good mantra meditation practice.

4

The Word

A mantra is a sacred word, the eternal Logos, that 'word beyond recall' of which the Psalmist speaks, vibrating in the universe. It is any word or phrase that enshrines the essence of that towards which we gravitate in the depths of our being, and which we call God. For the Hindu the most sacred of all names, the most sacred of mantras, is the word 'OM'. Many Christians do not understand this: I recall one brilliant Cambridge don, a Catholic, who dogmatically asserted that a mantra is a meaningless word.

Many adherents of the world's major religions put the power of the Holy Name into practice through the repetition of spiritual formulas containing a holy name or a divine attribute. The mental repetition of the Holy Name is one of the simplest and most effective ways of practising the presence of God. Mystics of all traditions testify that the mantra, systematically repeated over a period of years, can permeate our consciousness, transforming our character and enabling us to rise to the highest state of spiritual awareness. God has been called by many names in different cultures and times, but by whatever name He is called we are invoking the Lord of Love, the Ultimate Reality.

The Christian might choose as a mantra the word 'God', though many find the use of a familiar English word too distracting because of its academic, theological or childhood associations. They may therefore choose either a Hindu mantra, one of the sacred names of God, or use the Greek word 'Abba', which means the Unknown Origin as well as Father. Alternatively the sacred name may be incorporated into a phrase, as in the famous Hindu mantra, '*Om mane padme hum*'; or the Jesus prayer of the Orthodox Church, 'Lord Jesus Christ, Son of the Living God, have mercy on me'. There are many possibilities of mantras for the Christian. It can help to write out on blank sheets of paper such words or phrases that speak to us, and then to pin them up where we can see them as we go about our work. Gradually we may find one speaking to us more than another. Such phrases and words include:

I am in the Father and the Father is in me
I am the Son (Daughter) of God
I am the Light of the World
I and the Father are one
I am the Resurrection and the Life
I am the Way
Rest in the Lord
Yes!
Show me, Lord, your Way
Abba
Father
Lord Jesus
Most Sacred Heart of Jesus

Whichever mantra we choose – or, more accurately, whichever mantra chooses us (often a mantra will appear in a dream) – we must stay with it and not keep changing; we must not keep trying on mantras like hats. As the Jungian analyst Toni Sussman used to say, 'The easiest way to go into meditation is to have a mantra – out of that may grow a mandala. Whatever you receive will be in proportion to what you are fit to receive. One does not draw a mandala, one *becomes* a mandala. One does not hear or repeat a mantra. One *becomes* a mantra. One has to work. It does add up as you go on.'

We may find that for a period of time the mantra vanishes altogether and that there is just a stillness, a Zen-like emptiness, a total awareness at the centre, a hushed silence like that before dawn, and then, very softly, like a distant bell, the mantra is heard once again. In any case we must not become trapped by the word, by its sound, or by its associations. And if our mantra is a phrase such as 'I am the Way', the 'I' is that of the Eternal One, and we do not ourselves identify with it in terms of the ego. It is, rather, a 'greater than I who cometh after me'. We should not try to hold

onto the mantra with grim determination like a dog afraid of
losing a bone. Sometimes the beginner, like someone rattling
through a rosary, concentrates with a desperate ferocity upon
reciting the mantra as though counting up to a million. Nor
should we use the mantra in order to induce pleasant feelings, as a
process of self-hypnosis. Neither self-hypnosis nor desperation
will bring us to the heart of meditation, which is none other than
the union with the Divine, the Transcendent and the Immanent
God.

And here an important lesson has to be stated at the outset. We
cannot of our own volition, of our own action or will, arrive at
such a union. If we go to seek God we shall not find Him: that is
the paradox. It is God who comes to us: 'You would not seek Me
if you had not already found Me.' In meditation, in silent,
imageless, wordless prayer, the hardest thing is to let go of the
ego, to let go of the intellect, to let go of conscious control, to let
go of our feelings, and be open to the Spirit, listening with a
totality of response, surrendering ourselves absolutely to God
until we also can say with Simeon, 'Lord, now let your servant
depart in peace, for my eyes have *seen* your salvation.'

Time and again we create our own obstacles in prayer. In his
discourses on the *Atma Pooja Upanishad*, Bhagwan Shree
Rajneesh tells the story of a Zen nun who was carrying an
earthenware pot from the well. For thirty years she had been in
the monastry, meditating, making every effort to achieve tran-
quillity, but it had not come. Suddenly the water pot fell and it
broke. She stood there, seeing it shattered and the water flowing
out – and suddenly she was awakened. She achieved *satori*,
enlightenment. She ran and danced in the temple. Her master
came to her and said, 'Now you are a Buddha.' So the nun asked
how this was possible. For thirty years she had tried and it had not
happened. And on this particular morning she had decided that it
was absurd, that it would never come, and she had given up. So
why today had she received *satori*?

And the master replied, 'Because for the first time you were
total and without an ego. Effort creates ego. The very effort was
the barrier. Now without effort, without any motive, without any
ambition, you were just carrying a water pot and suddenly the
water pot falls, bang! and suddenly you become aware, with no

ego. And the very listening, the very breaking of the pot shattering, the noise, the flowing of the water, and you are there without any ego, listening totally – the thing has happened!'

One can easily become an 'expert', like those to whom I have already referred, who, after studying for a year or two in the East, return and set up as teachers, charging a lot of money for what was originally taught them free. Imitation is very easy: to achieve the authentic is arduous.

It can happen like this. Let us say that my mantra is the phrase, 'I am going into God'. Soon I will slough off the ego-centred part of this phrase in order to focus on the central action of movement towards God. In doing so I am not losing my own identity. I am not losing myself in God, risking inflation, risking the eventual statement: I am God. No. I know that I am I, but this awareness of myself is now in the background and the attention is upon the words and the reality behind the words: 'Going into God'.

The *Bhagavad Gita* contains these words: 'For on whomsoever one thinks at the last moment of life, unto him in truth he goes through sympathy with his nature.' Reflecting on these words, I recall a time when I was flying to America and the plane began to bump so much that I grew very frightened. Suddenly, quite spontaneously, I began to say over and over like a mantra the words, 'I am going into . . .' and there followed the name of the friend who is dearest to me in all my life. And with the repetition of those words I became calm and at peace, no longer afraid. I felt a sense of squareness, as of everything being in its proper place. Like a mantra? No, at that moment those words *were* a mantra.

If those whom we love can be so vividly present to us when we close our eyes, ought not God to be similarly present? He is, of course, whether we are aware of Him or not; and at that moment He was mirrored in the friend who has taught me so deeply about love. It is Love that draws us, as in the Sufi poem:

> I thought of You so often
> That I completely became You.
> Little by little You drew near
> And slowly but slowly I passed away.

And so we return to the words 'Going into God'. They are said over and over again, quietly, until they become the one word

'Going'. Then we move from the action of 'going' to the image of 'into' — as into the arms of our lover or beloved, as into the baptismal font, into the ocean, into flight like a bird: 'Our hearts, O Lord, are restless until they find their rest in Thee.' 'Into, into, into, into, into, into, into. . . .' And finally we arrive at the one word 'God', and that, repeated over and over, becomes our mantra, and now there are no more images.

God
God
God
God
God
God
God
God
God
God
God
God
God
God
God
God
God
God
God
God
God
God
God
God
God
God
God
God
God
God

5

Practice

Practice is the daily discipline, morning and evening. Whatever time we set aside, it must be observed as regularly as possible. If we have decided on twenty minutes at the end of each day, then it must not be allowed to shrink to fifteen minutes or be omitted because we are tired or choose to do something else. As we enter more into the practice of meditation so the amount of time devoted to it may increase, but in general, for most ordinary people leading full and demanding lives, both professionally and domestically, half an hour at each end of the day represents an ideal average. To spend more than this at meditation, unless under supervision, can be dangerous, leading to passivity, quiescence or complacency. The important rule is that, however busy and demanding our life, we can always make time and space for the needs of the spirit, although doubtless it may mean giving something up!

No one can be argued into a knowledge of God. Spiritual truth remains a revelation, a gift. The necessary condition of belief is the desire to believe. The coming of Christ, of the Truth, had to be preceded by the coming of John the Baptist. The way has always to be prepared and the ground tilled if the seed is to take root. In summer, especially, we see how very quickly a neglected garden reverts to being a wilderness as weeds flourish and grass grows high. It is only by constant weeding, mowing, digging, pruning and cutting back that we can hope to create and maintain order. That is why we have to give heed to the requirements of our inner life. It is no good waiting until we retire, thinking that then we shall have plenty of time for prayer. Lao Tzu says, 'Lay plans for the accomplishment of the difficult before it becomes too difficult.'

When we use the word 'practice' we tend to think in terms of doing something that will give us a skill. We think of developing specific talents. We go into training in order to achieve results. What is not realized in the West is that every action which is repeated over and over contains within its repetition the possibility of an inner perfection, so that walking, running, sitting, gardening – any action – can be the means by which we achieve an inner strength. In this way everything from gardening to cooking, from washing up to making love, from driving a bus to delivering the mail can become an opportunity for development along the inner way. This is what is meant by the Japanese saying, 'Archery and dancing, flower arranging and singing, tea-drinking and wrestling, it is all the same.' What ultimately matters is not what we get out of an activity, but what goes into it. Thus everything can become a meditation. And that is why, ultimately, at the eternal level, it is unimportant what we do in life. Everything – success or failure, great or small – contains within itself an opportunity for growth.

In *Sun Buddhas, Moon Buddhas* Elsie Mitchell tells a story which perfectly illustrates the Eastern approach to practice and repetition. Her roshi, Soen Nakagawa, poet, artist, and Zen master, once showed her some ink drawings. On each sheet of rice paper there was a painting, repeated a hundred times on each sheet. The figure was that of a Compassionate Bodhisattva. The figures were uniformly the same and yet it was possible to see that each figure, so deftly done, was different in some way from all the others. Each was unique and, tiny as it was, had a special strength.

'The lady who painted these few sheets,' explained the Roshi, 'has in recent years made many thousands of only this one Bodhisattva of Compassion. When I first met her she was a young girl, recently crippled by a dreadful disease which destroyed her ambition and opportunity to become a ballet dancer after the Western Fashion. Her parents were in despair because their daughter had become like a vegetable, and I was called in to talk to her. Of course I did not know what to say to such a young woman, but to please her parents I went to visit, and with me I took a calligraphy brush and rice paper. I drew for her one Compassionate Bodhisattva – then another, and then after that some more. Her eyes followed what I was doing and when I saw her interest, I took her hand and guided it until she was able to draw this figure by herself. Over and over she painted, and at each visit I told her what she had done was fine but she must do many more. She must do twenty-five in a day, then fifty, then a hundred, and so on like that until she was doing many hundreds each day. That was many years ago. Now she is a happy woman. She still draws the same figure but she can draw many others as well. She has talent; but most important she has discovered that this Bodhisattva, whom she has drawn so many thousands of times, lives in her own heart, as well as in the hearts of others who are not awakened as she is. She has kept careful account of the number of pictures she has made.'

The Roshi told her that each must be counted, that it was very important not to forget even one single figure. So on every page she wrote the exact number of Bodhisattvas she had drawn. 'The counting, the attention, is good,' observed the Roshi; 'one should see each thing as it is in itself in order to experience complete Buddhist awakening. However, it is not the counting which is most important. Counting or not counting is not the point. What matters is for each person to discover the Buddha heart in himself or herself. It is the discovery of the Buddha heart that really matters.

The ink-brushed mantra, like a mantra that is chanted, or that is simply absorbed during silent meditation, reveals its deepest meaning in the course of lifelong practice. What is important is the Buddha heart – or the heart of Christ.

Seated thus in meditation, whether that of the breath or that of the mantra, it is inevitable that thoughts and distractions will enter in to claim our attention. It is impossible to stop this activity, so we should allow them perfect freedom. We must acknowledge these distractions and gently return to the central stillness. Slowly we shall learn how to sit back and observe, like an angler on the bank, the rise of each thought, allowing it to sink back whence it came. The author of *The Cloud of Unknowing*, one of the outstanding spiritual treatises of fourteenth century England, speaks about the temptations which the devil puts in our way while meditating. However, in the early stages I doubt whether it is the power of evil so much as a subconscious resistance as we begin to reach down into ourselves and make contact with the divine. It is all too easy to blame the devil; it is we ourselves who are largely responsible for most of our problems, dilemmas and illnesses. There is always a resistance to change, both in society at large and within the society of our selves. Even the breaking of a simple habit is no easy task. Therefore, as we attempt in meditation to empty our minds of all thoughts, images and associations, it is inevitable that they will assault us with all the ferocity of the stones flung at St Stephen when he was being martyred; yet, like Stephen, we must keep our gaze heavenwards and, since the kingdom is within, inwards, upon the source of all Being.

We should not be surprised at what comes to the surface: what angers, lusts, obscenities, terrors and trivialities. We have to learn how to accept all these negative things inside us and, like Prospero in *The Tempest*, be able to say, 'This thing of darkness I acknowledge as my own.' The Venerable Chogyam Trungpa has described how, in the *Lankavatura Sutra*, the unskilled farmers throw away their rubbish and buy manure from other farmers, but those who are skilled go on collecting their own rubbish, in spite of the bad smell and the unclean work, and when it is ready to be used they spread it on their land, and out of this they grow their crops. That is the skilled way. In exactly the same way, the Buddha says, those who are unskilled will divide clean from unclean and will try to throw away Samsara and search for Nirvana; those who are skilled Bodhisattvas, however, will not throw away desire and the passions and so on, but will first gather them together. That is to say, remarks Chogyam Trungpa, one should first recognize and acknowledge them, then study them and bring them to realization. So the skilled Bodhisattva, rather like a person in analysis, will acknowledge and accept all these negative things. He knows he has all these terrible things inside him, and although it is very difficult and unhygienic, as it were, to work on, that is the only way to start. So out of these things comes the birth of the seed which is realization. 'And this is how one has to give birth, and the very idea that concepts are bad, or such and such a thing is bad, divides the whole thing. . . . If a person is skilled enough and patient enough to sift through the rubbish and study it thoroughly, then he will be able to use it. In this way you gain a complete understanding of what you are and that is more important than continuously creating.'

This is especially important for Christians, who tend to posit good and evil as opposites, perpetually in conflict, and do not understand that in our _shadow_ side is almost always hidden the seed of new growth. Good and bad, right and wrong, too often impede the spiritual growth of Christians. In the practice of meditation the question is not: Am I doing it right? Am I doing it wrong? In Zen archery it is not _how_ I hold the bow that matters, but the spirit in which I hold it. If I have decided that for me the practice of meditation is essential to my whole life; that, indeed, all my life is in the process of becoming a meditation, then I have nothing to do but meditate. It is not a matter of proficiency or skills, of right or wrong. It is the daily, hourly perseverance that counts, in season and out of season, being mindful and aware, resting in the presence of God, allowing my soil to be dug over by the action of the spirit and accepting all that will be excavated in the process.

It is like sitting out of doors on a sunny but cloudy day. Sometimes we feel the sun beating down on us and we bask in its heat. At other times the sun is clouded over, but we know that the sun is still there and that we shall feel its warmth again. We do not need to change our position. We do not worry. We wait. This is important. Sometimes all that our meditation seems to consist of is waiting, without sense, without achievement, often with a sense of unrelenting boredom, of futility and exasperation even, and deluged in filth. But it does not matter what _we_ feel or do not feel. We go on waiting on God. We surrender ourselves. We wait.

If we have a cold or are unwell, we should not strain. We should simply sit, accepting our unwellness or pain, not trying to deny, escape or forget it. Only in quietly accepting what we are shall we transcend our weakness. If we are frightened or in pain we should start the deep breathing again until gradually the fear or pain recedes. This deep breathing, this conscious letting go of the fear or the tension, can in itself be a form of prayer, and it assists the natural healing process. Similarly, if we are sitting with someone who is ill in hospital, and perhaps not even conscious, the act of breathing deeply in and out while holding their hand can become a powerful form of prayer and healing. Even in the

worst extremities of pain, as we breathe in and out, we have but
to murmur inwardly: 'Lord, I am helpless, help me.'

On some days the time set aside for meditation will seem
interminable. It can happen both to the beginner and to the
person who has been meditating for years. When this happens we
should not cut short the time set aside but, rather, open our eyes,
look at the clock, acknowledge our restlessness and then go back
into the meditation. Even if this occurs every few minutes there is
no need to be discouraged. One needs great patience in training a
puppy: great patience and, above all, great love. T. H. White in
The Goshawk, describing the training of that bird, observes, 'I
saw now that I must learn to feed him with diligent and minute
observation. Suddenly I realized that this was the secret of all
training.'

Seated in meditation, we keep before our inward gaze the
presence of God. As the unknown author of *The Cloud of
Unknowing* expresses it, 'His will is that you should look at Him
and let Him have his way.' To be still is truly to wait upon the
Lord. And just as a summer bluebottle will irritate and distract us,
so too will thoughts, worries and distractions break in to jar our
concentration. The actress Maggie Smith once said of an actor
whom I had to direct, 'He's like a bluebottle, all over the place.
You never know where he's going to be next, and he never stops
still long enough so you can swot him!' Each time the bluebottle
distracts us, we must disengage ourselves and return to that inner
gaze upon the Lord. As Lao Tzu wrote, 'I do my utmost to attain
emptiness. I hold firmly to stillness. Returning to one's roots is
known as stillness.'

Thoughts and images will arise. We must not strain to ignore
them but keep returning to our roots, to the point of stillness,
breathing in and breathing out, emptying our selves so that That
Which is Above and Beyond, Beneath and Within, may possess
us. However, some thoughts and images may arise which are not
necessarily distractions but which well up from within, or
descend from above, bearing messages and intimations: a phrase,
an idea, a plan of action, an image that is an icon. We should
neither resist nor reject such messages but let them rise to the
surface of our consciousness like fish, holding them momentarily
in our gaze, then allowing them to sink back into the pool of

silence. Later, outside our meditation time, we may choose to consider them further. They may prove to be valuable insights and inspirations. The river flows past but we remain on the bank. There is the river. There is the current ever flowing. There is the angler waiting. And the river and the angler are separate but one. The angler waits for the Great Fish.

Once, on a retreat I was leading at an old country house in Suffolk, on a cold day in March a group of us were sitting, wrapped in blankets, around a large ornamental pond in the garden. Our meditation was to gaze into the pool. In that pool the grey-blue sky was reflected, its stillness disturbed at first only by the passage of a bird in the sky, reflected in the water: a crow winging its way to the nearby wood. Then, beneath the surface of the mirror, among the dark roots of the water lilies, we became aware of a large goldfish moving slowly, appearing and disappearing. At the heart of every Pool the Great Fish lies waiting. But we cannot command him. He appears of his own will, and in the same manner he disappears. When the mirror reflects nothing but the empty sky, even then he is there, deep beneath the surface. We sat on, watching and waiting. We saw the mirror change colour as the sky became green and then, softly, out of the sky, snowflakes began to fall, and we watched these in the mirror. Snowflake after snowflake met its image and was dissolved in the Great Pool, becoming one with the Infinite. 'When you fix your heart on one point,' said the Buddha, 'then nothing is impossible for you.' At the heart of the Pool the Great Fish lies waiting.

In order to be able to persevere in the practice of meditation, we must feel that our present form of life is unsatisfactory, for only when a real need is present can prayer grow. Without need, without an ache of the heart, without a yearning of the spirit, without a hunger for the words of eternal truth, nothing new can come into being. And the more we open ourselves in prayer the more vulnerable we shall become, the more accessible to God's plan for us. If God is indeed an endless journey, then such a journey calls for an inner and an outer surrender of the ego and our own will. Only to the extent that we learn not to take ourselves as the measure of all things, not to assume that we are the masters or mistresses of our fate, and to realize that we are *subjectum Dei*, the servants and instruments of a higher power, can our practice of meditation be wholesome.

Our growth in the inner life with God will permeate everything we do, provided we will let it, and lead us into a greater awareness of our essential self. What we are doing is allowing God to work in us, to knead us with his own hands. We cannot see what he is doing, nor can we control what he is doing. If the metaphor may be changed, we allow ourselves to be shaped by the Master Sculptor, for only he knows the ultimate design. If at times he appears to be breaking us, we should remember that it is through the cracks that the light breaks through.

Courage and determination are needed. New things are always stimulating at the start but, as in the biblical parable of the Sower, many who set out on the path of meditation fall by the wayside as the going becomes difficult. There can be no real inner growth without great perseverance. If the mind is not fully attentive, if we attempt our meditation half-heartedly, the result will be grievous psychic and spiritual harm. Unless we are sure of our calling it would be better not to start; but, having once put our hand to the plough, we must follow the furrow.

> Look well, O soul, upon thyself
> Lest spiritual ambition
> Should mislead and blind thee
> To thy essential task –
> To wait in quietness:
> To knock and persevere in humble faith.
> Knock thou in love, nor fail to keep thy place before the door
> That when Christ wills – and not before –
> He shall open unto thee the treasures of His Love.
>   Father Gilbert Shaw

The Buddha is reported to have said to those beginning to meditate: 'Begin – and continue.'

Prayer cannot be taught by books. A book, a few words, perhaps only one phrase in a book, or a shared insight from another pilgrim, may act as a signpost, no more. Prayer, like art, must be experienced. You cannot know about love until you are in love. And just as we stand in front of a painting, or read and reread a poem, or hear and hear again a certain piece of music, and nothing happens, its essence eludes us; so, too, with God. We stand in front of a painting by Paul Klee or Stanley Spencer, trying to see something in it. There must be, we feel, something there; others have found it, and yet – nothing happens for us. We read a poem by William Blake or Gerard Manley Hopkins but remain outside of it. For some reason the door to the experiencing of that poem remains locked to us. Yet we know that there is something in the painting, the poem, the sculpture or the piece of music, and so we persevere. So, too, in the practice of meditation, we sit or kneel, turned in to God, but nothing happens. We remain outside a locked door. But, just as we keep returning to a particular painting or poem, hoping to find the key to it, we keep coming back to God in meditation and we wait. Then, one day, we share in the vision of the painter, the sculptor, the poet. A door inside us has opened and we enter into the landscape of the artist. So it is in prayer.

In *The Way of the Sufi* Idries Shah tells the story of the great Shibli who used to visit the illustrious Thauri. The master was sitting so still that not a hair of him moved in any way. Shibli asked, 'Where did you learn such stillness?'

Thauri replied, 'From my cat. He was watching a mousehole with even greater concentration than you have seen me.'

In these periods of waiting we should not expect to feel anything, nor should we look for results: otherwise we shall be like those lovers who are so unsure of themselves that they are always demanding assurances and reassurances, or like a nervous gardener who, having planted bulbs in the winter, is forever digging them up to see how they are faring. We are so accustomed to end-gaining that we find it very difficult not to be doing something. If we can fill our prayer time with devotional exercises and pious examinations of conscience, or rigorous practices, then we feel the time is justified. But in the life of prayer a vessel can only be filled when first it has been emptied. 'In the pursuit of the Way,' says Lao Tzu, 'one does less and less every day. One does less and less until one does nothing at all, and when one does nothing at all, then there is nothing that can be undone.' He is not saying that we should be lazy or totally passive: we must continue to lead busy, full lives, but when we go apart to pray we must learn to be still and to know God. And the more we practise, the more will this stillness invade our whole being so that, however busy or active our lives, there will be at the centre a stillness, an awareness, a listening.

Of course we can easily induce something to happen; it is perfectly possible in meditation, as in life, to attempt an assault on the citadel; to take up a mantra and repeat it with such ferocity that we shall experience either a blinding headache or else a release of emotion as exciting as a ride on a roller-coaster, or as calm and beatific as a trip in a rowing boat on an Austrian lake in high summer. And we may become very adept at inducing such states of euphoria, with only an occasional headache! The need for peace within is so deep, the desire for release from neurotic tension or the strain of overwork so great, that as soon as many people set the mantra in motion they become immersed in a feeling of peace and contentment, from which they emerge refreshed, charged with a new energy, cleansed and relaxed as from a sauna followed by a swim in a mountain pool beneath the first stars. All this is very beneficial as a simple form of therapy, but we must not delude ourselves into thinking of it as prayer. Such meditation is a natural technique, invaluable for releasing tension and tapping the essential wells of energy within each of us. Many doctors rightly recommend their patients to take up such a form of meditation, recognizing that their illnesses are all too often psychosomatic in origin – caused by stress and anxiety or guilt. Such a form of natural meditation is a beginning and can lead on to that encounter with God which is called prayer. In this higher form of meditation, however, we shall have to learn how to do without euphoria.

> I said to my soul, be still, and wait without hope
> For hope would be hope for the wrong thing; wait without love
> For love would be love of the wrong thing; there is yet faith
> But the faith and the hope and the love are all in the waiting.
> Wait without thought, for you are not ready for thought.
> So the darkness shall be the light and the stillness the dancing.
>   *East Coker*, The Four Quartets, T. S. Eliot

There is nothing that we can do except wait. Of necessity we all tend to live, work and think in terms of the ego: *I* live, *I* strive, *I* love, *I* pray; *my* wife, *my* husband, *my* children, *my* house, *my* ideas, *my* meditation – until at times the whole world seems centred in that *I* and all the world is *my* possession. If we try to fight against it, we only succeed in reinforcing the ego, which hugely enjoys saying '*I* am struggling to overcome *my*self.' But in meditation, in that form of prayer which consists simply of gazing at God ('I look at Him and He looks at me,' as the old countryman described it to the Curé d'Ars), Jesus says to the Martha in each one of us, 'You are troubled about many things. One thing alone is needful. Be still. And know that I am God.'

The world about us is visible to us. What we can see with our own eyes, touch with our own hands, we can verify, observe and draw deductions from; but the world invisible, the reality beyond this present reality, which we cannot physically see or touch – how to verify that? There is no way, scientifically or intellectually, that we can come by such knowledge, for it is knowledge of another order. No one can be argued into a knowledge of God. Truth remains a revelation. No one can be talked into falling in love. Love remains an experience. And in the silence of meditation there will come a knowledge that has nothing to do with questionnaires or encyclopedias; a knowledge that cannot be proved scientifically or even pinned down into words – and yet it is a knowledge of unshaken and unshakeable surety. To read all the books on prayer, to study all the various techniques of prayer, may be necessary on the way, but however wide-ranging our superficial knowledge of such matters, however articulate we may be in debate – even an authority on prayer – none of this will count if we do not have true knowledge. It is not necessary to 'know about' prayer in order to have a knowledge of prayer. This needs to be stressed, because many good people shy away from meditation or contemplation, assuming that this kind of prayer is for intellectuals or for 'religious people', and not for ordinary folk like themselves, having to earn a living and cope with noisy children, bills, neighbours, redundancy and other distractions.

Many shy away from wordless prayer because it represents a challenge, just as some people shy away from a commitment to love – and, of course, the two are the same. Then, too, people are frightened of silence because it means they have to come to terms with themselves. Our psychological development is linked to our spiritual development. A person who is ill at ease with himself or his many selves must deal with these problems first, needing perhaps the help of a counsellor or therapist. Whoever we are,

however, somewhere along the line we shall have to go into 'the
wilderness'. In 1960, when I was directing all six productions at
the Pitlochry Festival Theatre in Scotland, I went to stay on my
own for a week in a small guest house up in the hills. I was alone,
silent, thrust back on myself and forced to face my own
jealousies, insecurities, ambitions and terrors. It was a kind of
retreat, part of the continuing work on one's self, what Robert
Frost used to call 'time out for re-assembly'. Perhaps for this
reason I love the icon by John Rowlands Pritchard which hangs
on the wall before me now as I write: 'In the hills I study peace: I
visit and honour all sacred places: I hear the words of secret
silence.'

The wilderness into which Jesus went to fast and pray is also
symbolic of the waste places inside each one of us, of our own
wild and untamed natures, inhabited by the wild beasts of our
prejudices and passions. And we are called upon to smooth out
the rough places within ourselves, to make straight our own
paths. Jesus also commanded us to feed the hungry, clothe the
naked and forgive our enemies, but all our efforts for Oxfam and
world peace are of limited value if we neglect to clothe our own
spiritual or psychological nakedness, to realize our own hunger
and forgive our own selves.

We often say, 'Oh, I hate myself!', and our hatred of another
person is really the same thing. In savagely attacking another
person, libelling or slandering them, or judging them, we are
invariably attacking ourselves. We recognize in the other person,
although we do not admit – may not even be aware of – it, those
aspects of ourselves of which we are ashamed or of which we are
frightened, and with which we have not yet come to terms. We
say, 'Oh, she's so lazy, untidy, arrogant, uptight, domineering,
dictatorial, unreliable,' and so forth; and we fail to see that these
are our own qualities which we are, quite unconsciously,
projecting onto the other person. It is a common example of the
shadow aspect within each of us. It is only when we have learned
how to recognize it at work in ourselves and in others, and are
willing to learn from it, that we can truly learn to love our
neighbour as ourselves. It is only by entering into the labyrinth of
our own natures and by coming face to face with our own
monsters: our rooted prejudice, stubborn ignorance, repressed

sexuality, bigotry, resentments and obsessions, that we can hope to tame them. Then, after our forty days in the wilderness, alone with the wild beasts and the temptations, we shall, like Jesus, experience the angels ministering to us.

'Humility is nothing else but a true knowledge and awareness of oneself as one really is,' says the author of *The Cloud of Unknowing*, and, as T. S. Eliot reminds us, 'Humility is endless.' It is only when we have learned how to recognize ourselves in others, when we have learned how to forgive our own sins, feed our own hunger, clothe our own nakedness, love ourselves, that we can begin to love our neighbour. At the beginning of *The Tempest* Prospero speaks of his servant, the mis-shapen Caliban, as 'A devil, a born devil! capable of all!' How often have we said this of others? By the end of the play, however, he has learned to say, 'This thing of darkness I acknowledge as my own', and it is here, at this moment, that the monster Caliban is made to answer, 'Henceforth I'll seek for grace.'

Prayer will bring us to the very heart of the labyrinth. There we will meet the Minotaur. We will enter that labyrinth many times in our lives. Prayer is a paradox. It can be easy. It is easy. Yet it is also difficult. For the simple and uncluttered person it can often be easier than for the learned and sophisticated, who have first so much to unlearn. One thing prayer does demand: a commitment of love, a surrender of one's self. All the teachers in all the great spiritual traditions say the same. Once that surrender is made and we have crossed over the threshold, then Love will draw us on and in, whatever the difficulties we encounter or invent – for in the early stages of prayer the difficulties are nearly all of our own making. They stem from a false expectation of what prayer is about, just as the misunderstandings in our human relationships are all too often caused by unreasonableness, jealousy or romantic expectations which the other person cannot meet.

Another observation that can be made about the practice of meditation is that our generation is not accustomed to the idea of pain. At the first twinge we rush for the painkillers or, if we are hypochondriac, for the doctor. Yet many of our pains are clearly psychosomatic in origin rather than organic. If we can but accept pain, setbacks, opposition, misunderstanding, suffering of any kind, even active hostility, we shall learn from the experience, for

suffering brings both wisdom and compassion. Of course we
must seek professional medical advice for anything that seems
serious, but all too often our migraines, asthmas, hay fevers,
backaches, inflamed colons, sore throats, colds and many other
ailments prove to have a nervous, psychological or spiritual
origin. It may be that the body is protesting at our current
lifestyle, demanding that we slow down, listen inwardly, change
our diet, ease up on sexual activity, or make even more radical
changes in that lifestyle. Or there may be unresolved emotional
conflicts and unforgiven bitternesses that have been festering for
years. Sometimes our illnesses are caused by our very journey into
prayer, the body resisting the imposed stillness and trying to
distract us with migraines, headaches, sore knees and backache.
We have to learn to bear patiently the discomforts of prayer, the
physical aches, the appalling boredom, and those times when
body and mind protest at the stillness and emptiness, clamouring
that we give it all up. Just as the most loving relationships can
have their boring patches when we seem out of love with each
other and want to end it all, so too we are tempted to give up
praying.

We take no notice of such patches, other than to register, in
prayer as in love, that we are moving through a dry season. We
persevere in love, enduring the occasional pain and boredom, and
slowly build up a discipline that will enable us to endure rougher
weather and more violent storms. Thus, in time, as in those
human relationships over which we have laboured, we become
like a tree that has been battered by many storms but whose roots
go deep.

We have to work at everything, including love, both in our
relationships with others and in our relationships with God. Two
people who have lived together and loved each other over several
decades, who have gone on growing and developing, and are still
in love with one another and love each other, have a strength in
themselves as separate human beings and as a couple. Their
relationship is like a well-loved and welcoming house to which
others come for rest and refreshment. That is how our relationship with God should be.

Intermission

We are a house of prayer, prayer alone justifies our existence, and he who does not believe in prayer can but take us for impostors and parasites. If we were to say so more openly to the ungodly, we should be better understood. Are they not forced to recognise that belief in God is a universal fact? Is it not indeed a strange contradiction that all men can believe in God and yet pray to him so little and so badly? They rarely do Him more honour than to fear Him. If belief is universal, should it not be likewise with prayer? Well, my child, God wished it to be as it is, not making prayer, at the expense of our freedom, a need as pressing as hunger or thirst, but permitting that some of us should pray on behalf of others. Thus each prayer, though it be that of a little shepherd boy keeping his sheep, is the prayer of all mankind. *NB*

What the little shepherd boy does from time to time at the urging of his heart, we must do day and night. Not in the least because we hope to pray better than he – on the contrary. That simplicity of the soul, that sweet surrender to the Divine Majesty – which in him is a momentary inspiration, a grace and like to the spark of genius – we consecrate our lives to find or to recover if we have known it, for it is a gift of childhood which more often than not does not outlive childhood. . . . Once beyond childhood one must suffer to return to it, as at the end of a night one finds another dawn. Have I become a child again?

The Prioress of the Carmel at Compiègne speaking to Blanche, in the film scenario *Les Dialogues des Carmelites*, by Georges Bernanos, translated by Michael Legat

ACT THREE: The Journeying

Day 1

Place

A certain brother went to his Abbot and asked him for some words of spiritual comfort. The Abbot said to the monk, 'Go and sit in your cell. Your cell will teach you everything.' We read of Jesus that he rose early and went up into a high mountain, into the wilderness, into a lonely place, to pray. He went *apart* and prayed. So must we. Into a church or a temple or into another room, or on a bench in the park or in a square; even on a crowded train we can close our eyes and go apart.

If possible, too, that place apart should always be the same place. A space used regularly for prayer gathers to itself its own concentration. In a house full of children or other people this is not always easy. In India there is usually a corner of the crowded living room with a curtain drawn across it, where each member of the family withdraws to meditate. It does not shut out the noise but it does become a sacred place, a space apart.

Noise is a problem from which we cannot altogether escape. Our jangled nerves may cry out for quiet, so that even the ticking of a clock may cause us to wrap it in a scarf and place it in a drawer. Sometimes it may help to remove the immediate source of irritation, but we can become all too easily neurotic about noise when in fact the noise is inside us. If we can only sit there and accept the ticking of the clock, it will gradually merge into the background. Even if we do remove the source of one noise there will be others: a jet overhead, the squeal of brakes or revving of a car outside in the street, the voices of people next door, the blare of a radio or television. I was once at a conference of clergy involved in the media, for a meditation led by a so-called expert on the subject – he wrote, lectured, and broadcast on it. Yet he refused to start until a transistor radio playing outside the building was located and turned off. We had to sit there waiting until this had been done. Ironically, the song that was being played, and which could have been used as a starting point for the meditation, was the Beatles' famous song, 'Let It be'! I recall my friend John Hencher conducting a Eucharist, and right in the middle the telephone in the other room began to ring insistently. No one went to answer it but he wove into his spoken meditation an awareness of the outside world occasioned by the ringing of the telephone, so that the world beyond that room was caught up in that moment and in the eternal moment of the Eucharist. Gradually we shall learn how to let things be, to take these noises into ourselves while we are being drawn into a deeper silence, so that these noises are heard at a distance, and in time scarcely at all.

If we are interrupted in our meditation; if, for example, someone passes through the room, we should accept that interruption, even smile or make comment, not try to shut it out by becoming tense or pretending the person isn't there. Conversely, if we pass through a room where someone is meditating we ought not to be made to feel uncomfortable as though we were trespassing in a holy place. If the person meditating is truly indrawn then she or he will not be disturbed, and as we pass through we will absorb something of their calm, stillness and serenity.

> A man is meditating in a room. His wife enters to look for something. Man: Can't you see I'm trying to meditate? For Christ's sake, it's difficult enough without you barging in and out all the time!

In his small book *The Method of Zen* Eugene Herrigel describes a meeting with some colleagues shortly after his arrival in Japan. They were having tea together on the fifth floor of a hotel when suddenly a low rumbling was heard and they felt a gentle heaving underfoot. The swaying and creaking and crash of objects became more pronounced. Alarm and excitement mounted. The numerous guests, mainly Europeans, rushed out to the stairs and lifts. It was an earthquake; and a terrible earthquake which had happened a few years previously was in everyone's mind. Herrigel describes how he wanted to tell the colleague with whom he had been speaking to hurry up when, to his astonishment, he noticed that he was sitting, hands folded, eyes nearly closed, as though none of it concerned him. The sight was so astounding and had such a sobering effect on Herrigel that he sat down in front of the man and stared at him, without questioning whether it was even advisable to remain. When the earthquake was over – and it lasted a fairly long time – the colleague continued the conversation at the exact point where he had broken off, and without wasting a single word on what had happened. A few days later Eugene Herrigel learned that the man was a Zen Buddhist.

'Day after day,' says the *Bhagavad Gita*, 'let the Yogi practise the harmony of the soul . . . in a secret place, in deep solitude . . . with upright body, head and neck, which rest still and do not move: with inner gaze which is not restless but rests still between the eyebrows. Then his soul is like a lamp whose light is steady, for it burns in a shelter where no winds come.' Where no winds come. In that space or place of meditation there may be a meditation stool, a book, an icon or image. Like a church or temple, it will be a place set apart where we may rest in the Lord, be refreshed in the Spirit, and encounter the Divine. When we enter this place we may perhaps perform some simple ritual such as lighting a candle, or making a slow sign of the cross, which enables us to centre down before starting our meditation; it will vary with each individual. In general we should not tell other people or show them our place of meditation. Jesus is very clear about this. At such times our life is hidden with God. Yet we do not have to be pretentious or solemn about it. We will know, and we alone, that the source from which we draw is a deep underground river.

Day 2

Underground River

Sometimes when we are meditating it is as though we are at the bottom of a heap of rubbish, unable to lift ourselves up, so that a whole hour can go by in which nothing 'happens'. We seem unable to click into that alert and silent awareness of the breath coming in and out, the movement of the Pneuma. The time seems wasted. Sluggishness, inertia, apathy, a myriad distractions pile up on the roadside and block the way so that we cannot move forward. Yet we have already done the one thing necessary just by being there. Willingly and consciously we have set ourselves in the presence of God, even though He makes no sign to us of His presence.

When a friend is in distress, pain or need, and our presence is required, that moment may come when we ourselves are tired, distracted, preoccupied, ill or just not feeling up to the occasion. Yet our presence is all that is needed, however inadequate we may feel. We are present to share in and with a friend's pain, anger or loneliness. Similarly Jesus says to each one of us, 'Can you not watch with me one hour?'

We do not turn to prayer for comfort, though we may receive comfort in prayer. We turn to prayer to give comfort to Christ, to respond to his need, to watch with him one hour. We are asked to do so little for God. We do not even have to seek him, for we cannot find him, and he has already found us. In prayer we begin to experience that he is already there, that he sought us before ever we could seek him. And therefore, whatever we are doing, not just at prayer – he is there. This awareness of his presence is not an intellectual knowing but a total awareness. Jesus himself lived God so utterly – 'I am in the Father and the Father is in me' – and therefore for him every moment was an act of prayer, of being in union with God.

Even in sleep God is present. And even in sleep prayer can continue without interruption. If, as we lie in bed, we repeat our mantra, it will continue in our unconscious as we sleep, so that if we awake in the night we shall find the mantra continuing, and our whole being oriented towards God. The Psalmist understood this well: 'My eyes watch through the night to ponder your promise. . . . I will give no sleep to my eyelids till I find a place for the Lord. . . . My soul yearns for you in the night; my spirit within me earnestly seeks you. On my bed I remember you. On you I muse through the night.'

This secret life with God is like an underground river that surfaces on occasion and is glimpsed before it again goes underground and is lost to sight. We cannot see it, but we know that it is there. Like water diviners we sense its presence within ourselves and also in others. We know that it is there, even though others may doubt and challenge its reality. God is an underground river flowing to the sea.

> My River runs to thee –
> Blue Sea! Wilt welcome me?
> My River waits reply –
> Oh, Sea – look graciously –
> I'll fetch thee Brooks
> From spotted nooks –
> *Say* – Sea – Take *Me*!
>
> Emily Dickinson

The underground river flows through each one of us. When we have found a spring we sink a well; that well is prayer. But most of us, in the words of Karol Wojtyla (Pope John Paul II) are 'still far from the source . . . consider how arid, how arid, our souls'. In a long poetic sequence, *Song of the Brightness of Water*, he visualizes the meeting of the woman of Samaria with Jesus at the well, when Jesus said, 'Whoever drinks of this water that I shall give him shall never thirst.' The poet envisages the long night hours spent by Jesus in prayer, drawing strength from the deep well within himself. And yet how far most of us are from that eternal spring, and how dry our souls, he observes. We have so much to learn but it can only be learned by prayer, by the tiredness of hours of vigil, in the darkness alone with God, letting the eternal silence flow deep within us.

Brother Roger Schutz, Prior of Taizé, writes about this deep silence in one of his journals:

> Prayer, descending into the depths of God, is not there to make life easy for us. Prayer is not for any kind of result but in order to create with Christ a communion in which we are free. When man strives to give expression to this communion in words we have conscious prayers. But our understanding can only deal with the outer surfaces of ourselves. Very soon it comes up short . . . and silence remains, to such an extent as to seem a sign of the absence of God. Instead of coming to a standstill with the barrenness of silence, know that it opens towards unheard possibilities of creation; in the underlying world of the human person, in what lies beyond our consciousness, Christ prays more than we can imagine. Compared with the vastness of this secret prayer of Christ in us, our explicit prayer dwindles almost to nothing. Certainly the essence of prayer takes place above all in great silence.

Mother Teresa of Calcutta, a friend of Brother Roger, writes in a similar vein,

> We need to find God and he cannot be found in noise and restlessness. God is the friend of silence. See how nature – trees, flowers, grass – grow in silence; see the stars, the moon, the sun, how they move in silence. Is not our mission to give God to the poor in the slums? Not a dead God, but a living, loving God. The more we receive in silent prayer, the more we can give in our active life. We need silence to be able to touch souls. The essential thing is not what we say, but what God says to us and through us. All our words will be useless unless they come from within – words which do not give the light of Christ increase the darkness.

In prayer we have to learn how to go underground. On the Welsh border is an underground chapel: its flagstones rest directly on the earth, so that it always smells of earth and stone. Few people know of its existence, but those who need it find their way to it in silence. Light filters through small windows below ground. A large stone slab rests on oak supports for an altar. The crucifix hanging on the rough stone wall is by the American artist Meinrad Craighead, made when she was a member of the contemplative order of English Benedictines at Stanbrook Abbey in Worcestershire. The figure is of Christ in the tomb, and the Chapel is that of the Sleeping Lord. Descending the stone steps to the chapel, visitors have to bend their heads because of the low raftered ceiling, recalling the words of the Psalmist, 'Come in, let us bow and bend low, let us kneel before the God who made us.'

Kneeling in prayer in that chapel one is both in the womb with Christ and in the tomb with him. Here, among the green shadows, in the coolness, hearing the sound of birds and children at play in the garden above, these words resonate from an ancient homily for Holy Saturday, taken from the Divine Office: 'What is happening? Today there is a great silence over the earth, a great silence, and stillness, a great silence because the King sleeps; the earth was in terror and was still, because God slept in the flesh and raised up those who were sleeping from the ages. God has died in the flesh and the underworld has trembled.'

Often in this underground chapel I am again reminded of Abhishiktananda (Father Henri le Saux) in his cave in India.

> This hidden cave conveyed an amazing sense of mystery [an inner cave in the mountain of Arunachala, where a famous guru had lived]. It recalled all the old myths of the Earth-Mother: the fruitful source of life. One could only enter this sacred shrine alone and stripped of all clothing like a child in its mother's womb, and there, even more than in the central sanctuary of the temple, the whole mystery of rebirth was evoked, and that through signs which were so powerful that they almost seemed sacramental.

Leaving this underground chapel in Wales, ascending the steps to the enclosed garden, is like a death, a birth and a resurrection, especially after a celebration of the Eucharist there. And in the garden is a statue of the Risen Christ. For each of us, deep down underground, there is such a chapel where the deep river flows. Here, below ground, the seed stirs, sending forth roots, pushing up shoots and becoming the Tree of Christ. It has to be a secret growth, hidden away. There is no other way. All life is a sacred mountain filled with innumerable caves of prayer. All we have to do is to go into the mountain to find our cave and meditate there. The purest springs take their origins from deep within the mountain.

Day 3

Light

The miner with a lamp fixed to his head, enabling him to descend into the bowels of the earth and work his way along narrowing tunnels, chipping away the coal surface, is an apt image of the soul at prayer, recalling those portraits of St Dominic with a star just above his forehead, and reminding us of the Third Eye of spiritual perception. The motto of the Order of St Dominic is *Dominus, illuminatio mea* – the Lord is my Light. The Dominican Order has always placed great emphasis upon the light of reason and St Thomas Aquinas, the great theologian, was one of its most shining lights.

The Lord is my light and salvation. The light of reason can only take us so far, chipping away at the darkness. There is need, too, for the light within. The miner's lamp recalls also the wise virgins who kept their lamps trimmed, who were always in a state of waiting upon the coming of the Divine Bridegroom; and our experience will teach us that, in meditation, it is indeed as though at the very centre of our being a lamp were burning. All our attention and all our concentration are needed if that small flame is not to go out. It must burn calmly, steadily, a small flame in the surrounding darkness. It is a divine spark.

As the mind becomes stilled, so we begin to enter with deep concentration the inner sanctum of our being and of the Eternal Being. There the flame flickers like a tabernacle lamp. The ceaseless distraction of thoughts is like a draught threatening to extinguish it, but, as they recede there, at the edge of darkness, the light grows more steady; so that, even on those days when we feel nothing, when nothing seems to be happening, we know that far within, in the sanctuary, in the inner darkness, a vigil is being kept, and a lamp is burning. *Dominus, illuminatio mea.*

Day 4

Watching

In the Magnificat Mary tells how God has put down the mighty from their thrones and exalted those of low degree. Throughout the Gospels Jesus repeats that message: truth is seen as a paradox of seeming opposites. The American Shakers were known as the People Who Turned the World Upside Down, because of their radical beliefs, and all truth has an uncomfortable quality to it.

When Jesus in the wilderness has finished preaching to the five thousand he tells his disciples to give the people something to eat. They reply, somewhat tartly, 'We've only got five loaves and three fishes – unless you expect us to go out and buy food for this lot!' It is then that Jesus takes the unlikely loaves and fishes and blesses them and 'all ate and were *satisfied*'. Again and again it is as though Jesus wishes us to see that his truth is not the world's truth. Everything is turned upside down, inside out. We are challenged to examine everything afresh. The most unlikely means, the most unpromising people, are chosen. No wonder the disciples repeatedly had to ask Jesus to explain to them what he meant. He spoke constantly of those who have eyes and yet do not see what is in front of them, who have ears but do not listen. And in the parable of the Sower he showed how the ground must first be prepared before the seed can take root. So simple and so unlikely a form of prayer as this one of stillness, of doing nothing, is the means by which we too can prepare a way for the Lord.

It is very like birdwatching. We have to keep very still, waiting patiently, perhaps many hours, for the bird to alight or visit its nest. Often it will not appear, or we find that we have scared it away by a sudden movement. The prayer of stillness, of deep meditation, is such a waiting, a listening with half-held breath, for the coming of the Wondrous bird.

Day 5

Inspiring

'Come, Holy Spirit, our souls inspire and lighten with celestial fire!' Just as we give the kiss of life to a dying person, so too the Holy Spirit in meditation fills us with life, so that we become like a balloon being filled with air. If to expire means to give up the ghost, then to inspire is to fill up with the ghost – and ghost means spirit, the life-spirit. Thus, in meditation, spirit is put into us so that we are both in-spired and in-spirited.

A sensation of light will often come to us in our meditation. Sometimes it will seem to pierce the darkness like a blade, stabbing the heart with love. At other times our whole being will appear to be irradiated, flooded with light, and it will feel that we are being lifted up into another region, another time. Yet we must not seek after such experiences. They are not the reason why we meditate.

'Who is near unto Me is near unto the fire,' says *The Quest for the Holy Grail*. Too often we forget that the Holy Spirit is also fire. At Pentecost the Holy Spirit descended like tongues of fire, and Jesus also said, 'I am come to bring fire and what will I but that it be spread?' So, too, John the Baptist said, 'The one who comes after me will baptise you with the Holy Spirit and with fire. His shovel is in his hand and he will winnow his threshing floor; the wheat he will gather in his granary, but he will burn the chaff on a fire that can never go out.'

If we pray in earnest it will be with the realization that we are playing with fire. It is not merely, as all the masters warn, that we can get lost on the way, becoming inflated with spiritual pride and cut off from our fellow man, but also that fire, of its nature, destroys. The fire of the Holy Spirit will burn up all that is dross, much that we hold dear: our egotistical desires, ambitions, loves, indulgences. As St John the Baptist learned to say, so must we, 'As He grows greater, I must grow less.'

In these hours of silent prayer the Spirit will burn up the ego. When a garden has gone to seed it often has to be burned, dug up and all the roots removed; then, slowly and laboriously, that garden is recreated. Such prayer will make us more vulnerable, more open to wounding, as our roots are withdrawn. In the Garden at Gethsemane Jesus wept drops of blood because he knew that he had to surrender utterly his own will and be wounded even to death. However active our lives, in prayer we have to learn to be passive. Like Jonah we have to be swallowed up in the darkness of the whale before we can be reborn. 'Come, let us return to the Lord. He has torn us to pieces but he will heal us; he has struck us down but he will bandage our wounds; after a day or two he will bring us back to life; on the third day he will raise us and we shall live in his presence.' (Hosea. 6 vv.1–3.)

This long process of being torn apart will remove all likes and dislikes, all fierce attachments to this doctrine or that party. It will plant in us the tree of compassion. The mystery and the secret of Job is that, with courage and trust, he went right down into the burning fiery furnace, in which all categories are destroyed, and his last words are those of one who has *seen* something surpassing anything that can be *said* by way of justification: 'I have heard of Thee by the hearing of the ear . . . but now mine eye seeth Thee.'

Each of us is called to go on a journey. We can accept or we can refuse. If we accept, we enter upon a mystery of transfiguration which causes our familiar horizons to shrink. Old concepts, ideals and emotional patterns no longer fit, and we are challenged to cross over the threshold into that which awaits us beyond. Emily Dickinson, resisting the social *mores* and evangelical pressures of New England, understood this: 'I'm ceded: I've stopped being Theirs.' For each one of us, once that decision has been made – as all mythology reveals – there lies ahead of us a perilous journey before we reach the hidden treasure or elixir of life. But we shall not be alone. Just as Ariadne appeared to help

Theseus thread his way through the Labyrinth, so for each of us the ageless guardians will appear.

But if we refuse the summons of life, as Joseph Campbell observes in *The Hero with a Thousand Faces*, the adventure will turn against us. Walled in by boredom or unrelenting work, we lose the power of affirmation and become victims of life. The desert, instead of flowering, becomes a wasteland and life is meaningless. 'Whatever house we build in life will be a house of death, a labyrinth which shuts us in with our own Minotaur.' Those who are thus trapped in their own dilemma are like the souls in limbo to whom Christ shows himself in that homily for Holy Saturday quoted earlier:

> Truly he goes to seek out our first parent like a lost sheep; he wishes to visit those who sit in darkness and in the shadow of death. He goes to free the prisoner, and grasping his hand he raises him up, saying, 'Awake, O sleeper, and arise from the dead, and Christ shall give you light . . . I command you, Awake, sleeper, I have not made you to be held a prisoner in the underworld. Arise from the dead: I am the life of the dead. Arise, O man, work of my hands, arise, you who were fashioned in my image. Rise, let us go hence; for you are in me and I in you, together we are one undivided person.'

The promise is that, however deep our darkness, the light will find us out, and the smaller the crack the more powerful the beam.

Day 6

A Prayer

O Thou that art Beyond and Above,
O Thou that art Below and Within,
O Thou who *art* –
Scoop out within each one of us a hollow, a space, a place.

O Thou that art the eternal Fire, teach us so to play with Thee that
we may be burned of all that is waste.
O Thou that art the eternal Sea, O Thou from whom we come and
to whom we return, let Thy tides cleanse and renew us, sweeping
through the caves within.
O Thou that art the eternal Sun, rise up within each one of us, let
Thy light shine through the space that is within.

O Thou that art Fire, and Sea, and Sun, pierce our hearts of stone,
so that we may stand like statues against the sky, letting through
Thy light.

O Thou that art Beyond and Above,
O Thou that art Below and Within,
Shape us,
Hollow us,
Pierce us,
Divine Sculptor, until we stand in that image, foreseen from all
time, the image of our true selves in Thee.

To Thee, Sun, Fire, Sea and Wind, we prostrate ourselves,
                                   we lift up ourselves,
                                   we empty
                                   and
                                   we fill
                                   our emptiness.

NB !

Day 7

Caring

Milarepa, the Tibetan sage, warns, 'The concentration of inward quiet induces lassitude.' This is one of the dangers on the way and in the Way: that of quietism, of becoming so passive that meditation can begin to have as persuasive a hold as any drug. It is, psychologically, the call of the womb, inviting us to regress, to become as passive as a baby. Within such a cocoon we feel safe, secure, at rest in the Everlasting Arms. It is, spiritually and psychologically, a call that must be resisted as vigorously as did Ulysses the call of the Siren, even though it meant his being strapped to the mast of his ship so that he could not respond.

And among alien surroundings, among people to whom we do not immediately respond, whom we may even find antipathetic, it is dangerously easy to withdraw into this inward quiet. Some even use it as a conscious technique in difficult encounters, hoping thereby to discourage others, or as a way of avoiding painful but necessary confrontation. All such temptations must be vigorously resisted. When we are alone we may withdraw, but in the company of others we must always be present to them, *?* albeit with a stillness at the centre. We must be ready to respond to the needs of others, alert to act or, even more important sometimes, to react; ready to be shaped, affected – yes, even disturbed – by events; ready to risk upheaval.

Prayer for the Christian should, above all, result in a deepening awareness of others and their needs, a quickness to sense and respond before even a word is said; ready to stand alongside another in her or his suffering even though we may have no words to utter. Being present is what counts. Thus, through his prayer in a quiet and private place, the Christian should find himself more present in the marketplace. He should find the world in his heart. If he finds only himself then he is lost. 'I, if I be lifted up,' as Jesus said, 'will draw all men unto me.'

Even in the midst of much activity we can be listening inwardly. Do we pause at intervals throughout the day in order to rest, however momentarily, in the eternal silence? I often observe my gardener, Rob Rowe, doing this, pausing to watch the birds, or to reflect. He also teaches meditation, and for a day of walking meditation recently chose for his theme the saying: 'A Tree being motionless, birds come to it.' Do we reflect upon the rhythms and pattern of the day's events, its encounters and conversation, seeking for what people in the theatre call the sub-text, that which is not spoken? Even Quakers, curiously, are nowadays very loquacious outside a meeting for worship. You do not often encounter that once frequent, spontaneous, unaffected lapsing into silence, and thence into prayer, that was so marked a characteristic of Friends at one time. The Quaker journals of a hundred years ago contain many moving references to such occasions. A group of Friends might be sitting round the supper table, and one member discovered in silence with a look of gentle solemnity on her face. Gradually the others would become silent. After a while, the one whose attitude had initiated the spontaneous meeting for worship would convey a message that spoke to the need of the gathering at that moment. A period of silence would ensue, into which other thoughts or observations might be added, and then a final silence after which the general conversation would be renewed.

Silence can be positive; it can also be negative. There is the silence of resentment, of despair, of apathy, of non-commital. There is the silence when we cowardly opt out, refusing to speak, thereby condoning the evil of the situation. There is the silence of evil. There is creative silence, and there is also destructive silence.

Here is an image: the courtyard of an old country house in summer; swallows skim and arrow past; sparrows chatter on the drainpipe; woodpigeons coo murmurously in the woods; a stable clock strikes the hour; a bucket clanks; a dog barks. Yet nothing disturbs the sense of stillness of a hot summer's afternoon and the feeling of timelessness. Our thoughts and distractions in meditation are like the passing swallows, the chiming clock. We are aware of all these sights and sounds, yet in no way do they disturb or detract from that central calm.

> At the centre there is a silence.
> We descend into that silence.
> In descending we also ascend.

We are like the angels in Jacob's dream. Whatever experiences may be ours on the Mountain of Transfiguration there must always be a descent to everyday reality and the crowds in the marketplace. Often we may choose to end our meditation with a period of reflection upon those who invite our prayers. For a few moments, in quiet concentration, we hold each person in remembrance before moving onto the next.

The more we listen to the silence within, the more we shall begin to hear the silence in other people, to hear the things they do not say or cannot put into words. The Dominican motto is *Contemplare et contemplata tradere ad aliis*: to contemplate and, having contemplated, to pass on to others the fruits of contemplation. If we reflect upon the life of Christ we observe how the movement is continually between absenting himself to a lonely place to pray, and being in the midst of the crowds, in the marketplace, in the temple, accessible, at hand. We receive in order to give back. The measure of our prayer, as Christians, is the measure of our caring.

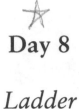

Day 8

Ladder

It is a common experience in meditation to have a sensation of light, like a shaft or a ladder, reaching down into the centre of our being. One of the earliest Christian martyrs was St Perpetua, who was killed along with her maid at Carthage in AD 203. She was twenty years old and a convert. While in prison she kept a diary in which she recorded her dreams, which she considered more important than her sufferings and which she felt were sent directly to her by God to give her courage and prepare her for the future. 'I saw a brazen ladder of wondrous length reaching up to heaven, but so narrow that only one person could ascend at a time; and on the sides of the ladder were fastened all kinds of weapons. Just beneath the ladder was a dragon lying in wait for those going up it.'

The image of a ladder recurs repeatedly in folklore and in the various cultural and spiritual traditions of mankind. In the Malaya Archipelago the Sun God is invited to come down to earth by means of a ladder with seven rungs. Some Malay tribes supply graves with upright sticks that they call soul ladders, inviting the deceased to leave their burial place and fly up to heaven. In their funerary texts the Egyptians preserved the expression '*asken pet*' (asken means a step) to show that the ladder provided for them by Ra to mount into the sky was a real ladder. 'I set up a ladder to heaven among the gods,' says *The Egyptian Book of the Dead*. A ladder with seven rungs is documented in the Mithraic Mysteries. An ascent to heaven by ceremonially climbing a ladder probably formed part of the ancient Greek initiation ceremony. Similarly in Islamic tradition,

Mohammed sees a ladder rising from the temple in Jerusalem to heaven. And in the Christian tradition the ladder is abundantly documented, the martyrdom of St Perpetua being but one example. The symbols of the stair, of ladders and of ascensions have been constantly employed by Christian mystics. St John of the Cross represents the stages of mystical perfection as a difficult climb; his *Ascent of Mount Carmel* describes the necessary ascetic and spiritual efforts in the form of an ascent of a mountain. There is also an early work on meditation by Guigo II, Prior of the Grande Chartreuse towards the end of the twelfth century, entitled *The Ladder of Monks and Twelve Meditations*, in which he uses the analogy of a ladder with four rungs. In some Eastern European legends the cross of Christ is regarded as a bridge or ladder by which the Lord descends to earth and souls mount to him, just as in Jacob's dream the angels descend and ascend. The ladder with seven rungs was also preserved in alchemical tradition. A codex exists representing an alchemical initiation by a seven-runged ladder up which climb blindfolded men: on the seventh rung stands a man with the blindfold removed, facing a closed door.

The myth of ascent to the sky by means of a ladder is also known in Africa, Oceania and North America. As Mircea Eliade says in *Shamanism: Archaic Techniques of Ecstasy*,

> If we try to achieve a general view of all the myths and rites, we are struck by the fact that they have a dominant idea in common: communication between heaven and earth can be brought about, or could be *in illo tempore* [the other time] by some physical means such as rainbow, bridge, stairs, ladder, vine, cord, etc. All these symbolic images of the connection between heaven and earth are merely variants of the World Tree or Axis Mundi. The myth and symbolism of the Cosmic Tree imply the idea of a 'Centre of the World', of a point where earth, sky and underworld meet.

In a monastery in the desert I once came across a chapel which had, on the wall behind the altar, instead of a cross or crucifix a silver ladder reaching up to the ceiling. Painted on the ceiling and the upper part of the wall were clouds, with light descending through an opening in the clouds. The only things visible in that opening were the soles of the wounded feet of Christ. They might have been the feet of the ascending Christ, or those of Christ descending at the end of time. Though what lies beyond is veiled in a cloud, in mystery, the way is open for that continual traffic between this world and the world that lies beyond and about us. Each time Mass is celebrated in that chapel and the Host is elevated, there above is the ladder that links heaven and earth through the very human feet of Christ.

In the *Aitrareya Upanishad* of the eighth century BC we read that 'Vamadeva having ascended aloft became immortal!' The ascension is indeed a very ancient symbolic doctrine, voiced also by Hindus and known to the Egyptian initiates. It was the supreme mystery which was kept secret in the Mystery cults of ancient civilizations. It is the meaning of Nirvana and of the Buddha's enlightenment, of union with God, the supreme religious experience. It is one of the great archetypes of the collective unconscious, common to all mankind. As Jesus said at the Last Supper, 'I am no more in the world and I come to Thee . . . I and the Father are One.'

Ascension and progression up the ladder are available to each and every one of us, only most of us prefer to remain clinging to the security of the known and established, in spite of the fact that this is contrary to the rules of creative living – 'I am come to bring fire.' Each time we go beyond ourselves is, of necessity, a painful experience. Each rung of the ladder is achieved with difficulty. It is like a succession of crucifixions together with a series of resurrections and ascensions within one lifetime.

When Jesus disappeared from sight, Luke tells us that the disciples returned to Jerusalem (the place of action) with great joy, 'and they were continually in the temple praising God'; while in the Acts we read, 'All these with one accord devoted themselves to prayer, together with the women and Mary, the mother of Jesus, and with his brothers.'

The foot of the ladder rests in the eternal sanctuary, and that sanctuary is within each one of us. We have but to kneel in prayer and He will descend to us and take us with Him.

Day 9

Faces of God

Job in his anguish cries out, 'Why dost Thou hide Thy face from me?' in the same way that the Psalmist repeatedly yearns for a glimpse of the Beloved, 'My heart hath talked of Thee, seek ye my face. Thy face, O Lord, I will seek.' And yet would we know the Lord if we were to see him? Do we, in fact, recognize him even in others – remembering his words, 'In as much as you did it unto the least of these you did it unto me'? *To the spiritual as well as the physical.*

The truth is that God has many faces, and some certainly we would not easily recognize. Too many Christians shirk the dark side of God, preferring an image of cosy sentimentality, neatly framed, like those anaemic portraits of St Francis of Assisi or of St Thérèse of Lisieux which belie the passionate reality of the person, their weaknesses and their strengths. It is well known that after the death of St Thérèse her sister retouched photographs of her, covering up the obstinate, self-willed mouth with a pretty, sugary, sentimental smile more fitting to the cult image of the Little Flower of Jesus. God has as many faces as his servants, but he also has a dark side which the Psalmist understood well.

> The Lord's voice resounding on the waters,
> The Lord on the immensity of the waters;
> The voice of the Lord full of power,
> The voice of the Lord full of splendour.
> The Lord's voice shattering the cedars,
> The Lord shatters the cedars of Lebanon;
> The Lord's voice flashes flames of fire.
> The Lord's voice shaking the wilderness,
> The Lord's voice rending the oak tree

> And stripping the forest bare.
> The God of glory thunders.

There was a period once when, for many months, at regular
intervals, the face of an Inca god used to appear to me in
meditation, not as a distraction but as a powerful presence. It was
in 1956 that I first saw this face. I was wandering in the Museum
of Natural History in New York and entered a hall where stood
this twenty-foot-tall stone carving of the face of an Inca god. I was
alone. As I approached, I experienced a powerful desire to
prostrate myself before it. When finally I departed I noticed that
the floor had been recently washed and there were my footprints
leading up to the base of that powerful, gigantic, stern stone face,
with its lidless, all-seeing and yet un-seeing eyes – like the eyes of a
Buddhist monk at prayer. Many years later that face returned to
me.

> 'I do not know why this face appears before me in meditation but I
> lie before it now, prostrate, without question. It is not evil nor does
> it threaten me. God has many faces and perhaps it is as well for us
> that we cannot yet see him face to face. If God really showed his
> face, our inadequacy would be revealed in one lightning glance and
> we would be blinded, destroyed. Perhaps he hides himself from us
> in order to protect us. We have to come to the Father of All Light by
> degrees. And what that light reveals, the face that will slowly
> emerge out of the many faces of God, may be, surely must be, not at
> all what we expect nor what we can surmise. No man hath seen
> God. Sometimes I think of the face of Christ when he drove the
> money-changers out of the temple; when he despaired at the
> stupidity of his own disciples, when he rebuked Peter. Those who
> saw his expression at such moments must have withered as did the
> fig-tree which failed to live up to Jesus's expectations of it.' (*From
> the author's New York Journal.*)

After all, what is God? Even St Thomas in the *Summa
Theologica* (1.12.ii) observes that God's essence cannot be
grasped conceptually. Perhaps that is why He appears differently
to everyone who approaches Him? In his autobiography Dom
Aelred Graham tells the story of a young man who visited the
community at Ampleforth and stayed for several days in discussion. When he came to say goodbye it was apparent that he
had been deeply impressed by the obvious unity, the manifest

spirit of charity, among the brethren. Yet one thing puzzled him. He had made a point of asking everyone he talked with about their notion of God. To his astonishment, although all had much the same background and training, revered the same religious tradition, professed the same faith, no two accounts of what God meant to the individual were the same. Subjectivity controlled the experience of each.

It follows from this that when we speak of God we are always speaking of ourselves – or, rather, of the Self that is within; and always we know, by a person's tone of voice, by their gestures and their actions, whether God is in them or not. God has ten thousand faces, and yet there is but one face. Faced with this experience of God, theology and doctrine are placed in true perspective.

All we can do is be in love. To be in love is to make an act of faith. We become what we love, and if we truly love then our beloved may be a thousand miles or a thousand years away, but slowly our life is changed.

Day 10

Opening

The practice of meditation leads us to an awareness that within each one of us is another landscape: it is like a country house with many rooms and attics, passages, gardens, woods and waste-lands. We shall become familiar with some of these rooms, many of which will be entered for the first time while others remain locked – at least in this existence. But meditation is not a guided tour of a country house. We do not set out to be self-indulgent, nor to spend our meditation time in self-analysis. It is, rather, that the practice of stillness leads to an increased awareness of ourselves (and of others), to a greater humility and sense of humour. Those last two points are important. All this talk, all the words in this book, can make us over-intense, a little too solemn, perhaps even precious, taking ourselves just a bit too seriously. It is essential to keep in touch with the *humus* or soil of reality. To be related to the *humus* will beget *humility* and true humility ripens into *humour*. We become less and less deceived about ourselves (and those selves are many), we have fewer illusions and therefore are more aware of other people as themselves and not as the carriers of our psychological projections. We become aware that many of the rooms within are shabby, shoddy or pretentious, while others, long untouched, when they are opened up and the shutters are drawn to let in the sunlight, prove to contain unsuspected treasures. In such rooms we discover unlived lives, unused talents and much neglected business.

The stone which the builders ignored proves time and again to be the cornerstone we need. Deep meditation is one such stone. When people feel frustrated and restless, finding no satisfaction in their work or their religion, their relationships deadlocked, they will still continue to do everything except this one thing: to be still and do nothing. They cannot conceive that doing nothing can achieve anything, so fixed are they in their prejudice that only *I* can help myself. And in the meantime the true Self lies neglected, that Self which has unsuspected powers of renewal. 'It is not,' says *The Cloud of Unknowing*, 'what you are or have been that God looks at with His merciful eyes, but what you would be.' We stand at the door of our own house. We have but to knock and let ourselves in.

The capacity of the human spirit for renewal is endless. Meditation is very like the creative process: the artist experiences periods when no inspiration seems forthcoming. For Robert Frost, the American poet, it once lasted ten years. But, from experience, the artist knows that these are fallow periods. Although the surface appears barren, as blank as a field or a garden in November mist and rain, he knows that underground the plants, roots and bulbs are biding their time. Knowing this does not make the dark days of winter pass more quickly; and the artist, unlike the gardener or farmer, will often experience despair born of the fear that perhaps the sources of his creativity have dried up. Yet even the farmer is at the mercy of the elements. 'Be patient, then, my brothers, until the Lord comes. See how the farmer is patient as he waits for his land to produce precious crops. He waits patiently for the autumn and the spring rains. And you also must be patient.' (James 5: 7–8)

Yet for the artist, and for the person who meditates and prays, wisdom (always the fruit of experience) teaches this patience. The spring does return in due season, though when it does come it may be an entirely new growth and not what we had expected.

> Who would have thought my shrivell'd heart
> Could have recovered greeness? It was gone
> Quite underground, as flowers depart
> To feed their mother-root when they have blown;
> Where they together
> All the hard weather,
> Dead to the world, keep house unknown.
>
> George Herbert

I recall being in Finland, working at the National Theatre, throughout one March. Towards the end of the month the thaw of the long winter snows began. This was a time of ugliness in Helsinki, with soot-coloured snow, sleet and puddles and dark, crow-black buildings. In the parks, as the last of the snows melted in the sun, I saw underneath the crushed and anaemic grass, as drained of colour as the whitened face of the 'winter' Finns who, daily now, assembled on the steps of the cathedral in the middle of the day to stand with eyes closed and pale faces uplifted to the returning sun. Yet I knew that within a short space of time the grass would spring up, green and vivid in the spring sunshine, just as those pale faces would turn golden and become the faces of 'summer' Finns.

Time and again it seems as though we will never recover from certain experiences that have battered us into defeat. Repeatedly in meditation it will seem as though the interior winter has no end. We sit alert, watching, yet the weather never changes. We begin to doubt the efficacy of what we are doing. Gone are the days of warmth, of glowing devotion, of beatific experiences, of being on fire with love. We have become a bleak and wintry landscape.

The artist knows, however, that underneath, in the unconscious, seeds are stirring. Then the day comes that a new work is created. And we, also, one day look up from our meditating and are aware that, quite suddenly, we have moved. Certain problems have fallen away from us, certain attitudes or prejudices have shifted and changed. A new awareness is born. If we really allow the creative forces their freedom (the Spirit blows where it wills) and willingly suffer the ignominy of knowing that, at such a time of winter, there is little we can do other than go on meditating, then it will take care of itself. Jesus said, 'It is good for you that I go away.' Winter is necessary to spring. All spiritual masters say the same thing, that such periods of bleakness are a testing; as Prospero says to Miranda in *The Tempest*,

> All thy vexations
> Were but trials of thy love, and thou
> Hast strangely stood the test.

Day 11

Falling

We should not be distressed by lapses from grace. They may well be necessary. We may have been trying too hard and so need to let up for a while. Or we may have become too inflated by what we imagine as our progress, so that a fall from grace jerks us back to earth, to the *humus*. It is like the game of Snakes and Ladders. Meditation is an ever-renewed struggle; time and again we slide to the bottom of the ladder. Of course, if we concentrate on winning, the game will seem even more pointless, more frustrating. We do not play to win, not in this game.

Once in a year perhaps, in the game of Solitaire, all the marbles disappear until only one is left in the centre. And we gaze at the circular board and the single marble and rest content. It is like what Zen masters call a moment of *satori*: a sense of having broken through, of union with That Which is Desired, when everything seems to fall into place.

It is often after such an experience that we fall most lamentably from grace. 'It had been a splendid day,' wrote T. H. White. 'He would go back. He was sure to. Goshawks, and this was the second time I had learned from experience, went back two paces every time they went forward one. "There is no short cut", said the good book, my manual, "to the training of the Goshawk." '

Day 12

Weeding

Wales, 3 August 1972

Unthreading clover roots on the lawn, raking them over in order to expose them to the blades of the lawn mower. Digging up the couch grass, delving deep with bare hands as in a bran tub and tugging out the white, stringlike roots, attempting to unravel them. It cannot all be done in a day. Once, like my father, I would have charged at the task, trying to tame the wilderness by assault, going on working for long hours, hoping to see order arrive out of chaos by nightfall. Now I am more patient. I try not to seek or see the end. Just so much a day. Creating *some* order.

I allow certain areas of wilderness, weeds and nettles, because I will never be able to tackle it all. Yet that very disorder, that patch of untidy garden, creates its own beauty and becomes a breeding ground for moths and butterflies.

I work slowly, creating a little order as I go, just keeping the wilderness at bay. I have a plan for, a vision of, this garden, how I should like it to be, but in order to achieve this I would have to live here all the time and that is not possible. Therefore, in that marvellous phrase of Mother Teresa's, I do what I can.

This garden is like my life. Is each person's garden so? In which case mine will never be finished. I shall die with the weeds still rampant. But where the weeds and nettles grow, there will be butterflies – Peacocks, Small Tortoiseshells, Red Admirals and Painted Ladies.

Remember the lawn in Notting Hill Gate.

Day 13

Garden

'And in the garden secretly. . . .' We spend our lives seeking the way back to the Garden in which man and woman first existed in perfect harmony with the Divine. It is a costly journey, and on the way other gardens have to be entered – the Garden of Gethsemane and the Garden of the Tomb.

Early on the Sabbath while it was still dark, Mary, who loved him so deeply, so passionately (Judas was shocked at the excess of her love) came to the tomb and was distressed to find it empty, the body gone. 'They have taken away my Lord and I don't know where to find him.' She was overwhelmed, as we so often are, by grief, anger, bitterness – engulfing us so that we can no longer see what or who is standing right in front of us. 'The meaning has gone out of our lives,' we cry. 'There is no sense any more! We are lost, and the one person, the one love, that did make sense of it all has been cruelly snatched away, even his body, even the memory of that love.'

Very quietly the voice speaks to us: 'Why are you weeping?'

And we reply to that voice, not even recognizing it, 'Because my life is empty! And I no longer know where my love, my life, my Lord is!'

Then it is, in that hushed garden, as dawn is breaking, the sun inching up over the hills and the first birds singing, that the voice speaks our name, so softly, in the stillness, saying: Mary, James Kathleen, Hywel, Franz, Jerome, Cynthia, Catharina. . . . That voice speaks our name as no one else will ever speak it or can say it, and we know then that we are recognized. He, whom we thought we had lost, has found us, and he knows us as we truly

are, who we are, what we are capable of and can be. He sees us in
the fullness of being, as we yearn to be, stumble to become. And,
with Mary, we cry out to him with joy, we reach out with our
arms to enfold him, saying, 'Master, Friend, Beloved, Rabboni!'

In life there are very few who love us in our totality of being,
even among supposedly close friends. Most people love us for
themselves because we mirror them, gratify or complement them.
When we fail to measure up to their expectations of us they cast
us away, reject us, savage us in their disappointment. It is never so
with the Divine Lover. He embraced them all in their weakness,
their vanity and unbelief, from Peter to Thomas to Mary. He
embraces us.

Here is a meditation with a difference, for a special occasion,
perhaps when we are especially troubled or desolate and unable
to see beyond our pain. If the house or apartment in which we live
is crowded, let us go for a walk and find a quiet place where we
can sit with closed eyes. Sitting there, in a city square or a field, we
imagine the garden of our dreams: it may be a particular garden
of our childhood, a garden we have known or visited, or it may be
a garden of our imagining. It may be a garden like King Arthur's
island valley of Avalon in Tennyson's poem *Morte d'Arthur*:

> Where falls not hail or rain or any snow
> Nor ever wind blows loudly, but it lies
> Deep meadowed, happy, fair, with orchard lawns
> And bowery hollows crowned with summer seas
> Where I will heal me of my grievous wound.

In our imagination we see the garden very clearly, we walk in it,
discover its trees, flowers, rocks, water; we listen to the secret
sounds of the garden, until it is all there in our mind's eye. And
then, still with our eyes closed, we find a sheltered spot in our
imagined garden where we can sit and wait for our beloved to
come. In the hush of dawn, or the quiet of dusk, we sit and wait
for him, and when he speaks he will call us by our name: Mary,
James, Kathleen, Hywel, Franz, Jerome, Cynthia, Catharina. . . .

The message of the eternal garden, of the garden that was in
Eden, the Garden of Gethsemane, and the Garden of the Tomb, is
one of love. Love is the key that will unlock the secret garden
within each of us. Love sharpens the perceptions; love fuses the

vision. We only live truly, we only live fully, when we love truly, love fully; when we are in him and he is in us, beyond all clutter of dogma and rules. To love is to live. It is the only way of living. When we find ourselves fulfilled in him, then our true selves will be realized. It is no wonder that Mary ran from the garden, crying, 'I have *seen* the Lord!'

Day 14

Doors

A Dream

I move in a landscape of tall doors in a vast space as high as the sky. They are not doors in the accepted sense. They have no top, there are no handles, they have no other delineation than formal steps ascending to each. They are doors carved out of rock, massive and immovable. How could I ever hope to open even one? To what realms do these doors lead? How to enter them all? Slowly there comes the realization that they are not for entering by myself but are for admitting others to this place in which now I stand.

'They are the doors of many possibilities,' says a voice. 'But only one or two will open for you. If you are patient then the intended opportunity will appear.'

Footsteps echo. The only other sound is that of many sighs. These are the sighs of those who did not wait and so missed their opportunity. They are the sighs of those who know that they can never pass this way again.

(from the author's Journal)

Sometimes we find that the door which we are convinced is ours will not open, or, if opened, leads only to an empty space; or else we find that one room leads to another, door after door, until we are hopelessly lost. Sometimes we hear lilting music, laughter and voices from behind a particular door and we long to enter; perhaps we even force our way in, only to be thrown out, hearing the door close behind us with a resounding and final bang. At other doors we knock and knock, bruising our knuckles, exhausting ourselves, until finally we give up in despair.

The poet John Keats understood about doors; in 1818, while staying at Teignmouth, he wrote to a close friend:

> I will put down a simile of human life as far as I now perceive it. I compare human life to a large mansion of many apartments, two of which I can only describe, the doors of the rest being as yet shut upon me. The first we step into we call the Infant or Thoughtless chamber, in which we remain as long as we do not think. – We remain there a long while and notwithstanding the doors of the second chamber remain wide open, showing a bright appearance, we care not to hasten to it; but are at length imperceptibly impelled by the awakening of the Thinking principle within us. – We no sooner get into the second chamber which I shall call the Chamber of Maiden Thought, than we become intoxicated with the light and the atmosphere, we see nothing but pleasant wonders, and think of delaying there for ever in delight: However, among the effects this breathing is father of is that tremendous one of sharpening one's vision into the heart and nature of Man . . . of convincing one's nerves that the world is full of Misery and Heartbreak, Pain, Sickness, and Oppression, whereby this chamber of maiden thought becomes gradually darkened, and at the same time – on all sides of it   many doors are set open – but all dark – all leading to dark passages – we see not the balance of good and evil, we are in a mist – *we* are now in that state, we feel 'the burden of the mystery'.

Jesus said, 'Seek and you shall find, knock and it will be opened unto you.' But many say, 'What mockery is this?' So many failures, so many heartbreaks, so much despair and pain, so many betrayals and disappointments, and, finally, after so many locked doors, or doors leading nowhere, the one door that always opens is that of death! As the Duchess of Malfi cries out, 'I know death has ten thousand doors for men to take their exits.' How can he say, 'Knock and it will be opened to you'? In every part of the world there are those who cry out, 'We also have been disappointed, betrayed, broken, crippled, destroyed; no doors have opened for us, and in the night we cry out on our lonely beds, "My God, my God, *why* have you forsaken me?" '

For the disciples after Calvary it was as though a door had slammed in their faces. They too were broken, disillusioned, downcast. They too were faced by that final door in the death of their Master. Three days later, Easter morning was to change all that. What is strange today is that, in spite of Easter morning, so many Christians are afraid of death, unlike the Hindus or the Buddhists. It is in part because too little is taught about the sacrament of dying, and also because we use the noun 'death' and the adjective 'dead', with their harsh and final sounds as of a prison door closing upon us. Yet death is but a transition. We pass through a door from one space to another. It is a moment of nature, so that we would do better to use the present participle, 'dying'. We die but to be reborn. And exactly how we go through that last door, how we die, will depend on how we respond to the many hourly, daily, yearly experiences of dying that we encounter in our lives, how we respond to the dying of a hope, a dream, a friendship, an ambition, a passion. If we learn how to live through each of these miniature deaths, each lessening of the ego, then each of them will become a resurrection, and so we shall come at last to those ten thousand several doors with joy and gratitude, humility and trust. If, on our journey down the years, we do this, then we shall also hear, increasingly nearer, that music from another room which is the life that is beyond and yet is all about us even now. And if, continually, hourly, daily, yearly, we learn how to die and be reborn, then we shall find that after long searching a door opens and there is a way ahead when we had thought no door would ever open for us. It may not be the door we expected, nor the door we would have chosen for ourselves, but it has opened and we have but to enter.

Each of us has to learn how to wait in order for our door to open. Too often we are seeking the wrong door and, like Emily Dickinson, we find ourselves 'looking oppositely for the kingdom of Heaven'. One door closes and another door opens. The truth is that the door which is most uniquely ours has been there all the time, only we could not see it. The disciples on the road to Emmaus experienced this, and for them, as for us, time and again, the Transcendent One, the Living Christ, is walking by our side – only something prevents us from seeing Him. We are so close to our pain, anger, lust, ambition or ego that we cannot see truly or clearly.

Although a few people seem to know from the start where they are going, most of us have to learn to wait for our door to reveal itself. One thing, however, is certain: when we find the door that is meant for us from all eternity we shall recognize it and it will open. Sometimes it is only towards the end of this existence that we recognize him, the stranger who is yet closer than breathing: when it is getting dark and night is coming on that we say to him, 'Abide with us, for it is now late.' And then it is, so late in life but never too late, that, like Cleophas and his friend, we invite him into our homes, into our hearts and into our lives. It is then that we know him, as we sit down together and break the bread of friendship for, as Keats wrote at the end of that letter, 'Your third chamber shall be a lucky and a gentle one, stored with the wine of love and the bread of friendship.'

When the door opens we can have little warning as to what form it will take. It may be, as for Karol Wojtyla, a lofty and mighty door of resounding bronze opening upon an awesome responsibility as Pope, or it may be a small door, so small that we have to go down on our hands and, above all, on our knees, if we are to enter it.

Thus after all it is true: Seek and you shall find. We have but to seek God and we have already found him, for it was he who first sought us and it is he who is the door. The door, whichever door, leads straight into his presence. There are many doors and yet there is only ever one Door. To each and every one of us he says:

> I am the Way – walk me
> I am the Truth – sing me
> I am the Life – live me.

Day 15

Lazarus

'If Thou hadst been here my brother would not have died!' says Martha to Jesus. Is there not within each of us a Lazarus in danger of dying because God is not there? Dying through lack of a continuing and continuous awareness of the presence of the Eternal Being? And is it not to each of us that are directed those words of Jesus, 'Lazarus, come forth!'?

It is we, already beginning to smell, who must come forth from the deadness of our own interior decay. What is the nature of this decay? In *Psychology and Alchemy* Carl Jung writes,

> The divine Mediator stands outside as an image, while man remains fragmentary and untouched in the deepest parts of him. It may easily happen therefore that a Christian who believes in all the sacred figures is still undeveloped and unchanged in his inmost soul because he has 'all God outside' and does not experience him in the soul. His deciding motives, his ruling interests and impulses do not spring from the sphere of Christianity, but from the unconscious and undeveloped psyche, which is as pagan and as archaic as ever. Not the individual alone but the sum total of individual lives in a people proves the truth of this contention. The great events of the world as planned and executed by man do not breathe the spirit of Christianity but rather of unadorned paganism. These things originate in a psychic condition that has remained archaic and has not been even remotely touched by Christianity. The Church assumes, not altogether without reason, that the fact of having once believed leaves certain traces behind it, but of these traces nothing is to be seen in the march of events. Christian civilisation has proved hollow to a terrifying degree: it is ... a veneer, but the inner man has remained untouched and

therefore unchanged. His soul is out of key with his external beliefs; in his soul the Christian has not kept pace with external developments. Yes, everything is to be found outside in image and word, in Church and Bible, but never inside. Inside reign the archaic gods, supreme as of old; that is to say, the inner correspondence with the outer god image is undeveloped . . . and therefore he has got stuck in heathenism. Christian education has done all that is humanly possible, but it has not been enough. *Too few people have experienced the divine image as the innermost possession of their souls.* Christ only meets them from without, never from within the soul; that is why dark paganism still reigns there.

Lazarus, come forth!
In the test of the Chester Mystery Plays, just after the raising of Lazarus, Jesus says to his disciples, 'Loose him and let him be!' This is what the Buddha ('Be ye lanterns unto yourselves') as well as Jesus ('Work out your own salvation in fear and trembling') would have for each woman, each man: that we be set free and allowed, each one of us, to be her or his own unique Self. Let her be. Let him be. Made whole. Repeatedly in the Gospels Jesus says to people after healing or making them whole, 'Go, and . . .', and there follows a practical command, something that each person has to go and do. It is as though He is saying to each one of us: 'Go, you have your freedom, now you know who you are, and you have a task to do. Go and do it!'

We may be versed in the Bible and able to explain that the incident is placed where it is as a prefiguration of the resurrection of Jesus. But, as with every incident in the Gospels, there is also the challenge: have we lived it in our own lives? Until we have been Lazarus and heard His voice summoning us out of our sleep, our apathy, our decay, we have no right to speak. Until the divine mediator stands within us, until we are touched in the deepest parts of our being, we cannot call ourselves Christians. Thou, O Lord, art in the midst of us, and we are called by Thy Holy Name.

'I command you, Awake, sleeper! Arise from the dead. Arise, O man, work of my hands, rise and let us go hence: for you in Me and I in you, together we are one undivided person.' Months, years go by and we remain locked into situations, imprisoned by our own wills, egos and prejudice. Embittered, opinionated, judgemental, resentful, jealous, envious, we refuse to let go of our chains. We prefer to blame others rather than ourselves. We refuse to make the first move, to forget the past, swallow our pride, laugh at our vanity and our tantrums, rise above our jealousies. We justify our actions, dressing them up in moral judgements. It is no wonder that we begin to smell of decay. We live in a house of death, draped in negativity. Some people become so negative that they cast a blight on all who are near them; every shining, positive, joyous initiative is blocked. Such people, it would seem, are not only on the side of death – they are already dead, as dead as Lazarus seemed to the disciples.

Yet change can come even as we lie dying. What is strange about Lazarus is that we have no record of what he said. He came back from the dead, yet he has nothing to say. There is a profound silence here. Perhaps that silence is the most eloquent thing in the whole story.

Day 16

Threshold

'In meditation the "fountains of the Great Deep" open and the region of the inner being appears. Here, in the silence of our aloneness with God, we learn the ultimate truths for which there are no words.'

K.O. Schmidt, *The Message of the Grail*

A threshold is a place of coming and going. A threshold is a frontier which challenges us to cross over or return. At a frontier we have to declare our identity. We may choose not to venture further and instead return home; or we may cross over into a new awareness, into a new dimension of reality.

I first learned about this from the sculptor Barbara Hepworth. She was speaking to me about doors, telling me how, when she designed an abstract set for the world première of Michael Tippett's opera *A Midsummer Marriage* at the Royal Opera House, Covent Garden, Tippett kept asking for real doors. 'I tried to explain to him that a door is a symbol. It represents a frontier. There is the journey to the door, then the pausing at the threshold, making a decision; and, finally, the crossing over into the other region, or else returning to base.'

In his diary Dag Hammarskjold, former Secretary General of the United Nations, often spoke of 'the frontier of the unheard-of'. Prayer is such a threshold, such a frontier. And in prayer, paradoxically, we ourselves are the frontier. As the breath comes in, goes out, we become aware that 'I am the Way'.

Prayer is as natural as the air we breathe, and as necessary. When a person who has never consciously prayed in his life begins the practice of prayer, he feels as though he is being restored to life. As the Spirit enters, so he is filled with creative energy and grace. He becomes a new man. Prayer is the kiss of life to a drowning person. The word 'air' means also a melody in music, as when we speak of 'Brother James's Air'. Prayer is that harmony of the spheres to which Shakespeare so often refers. Prayer is like a seashell; we have but to place it to our ear and we hear the music. 'I am the song – sing me! I am the tune – play me!' are words from a song of Neil Diamond's. In prayer we allow the song of the universe, the music of the divine Orpheus who is Christ himself to be heard. We become that music. Brother James becomes his own air. The state of being at the Threshold is one of watching, waiting and listening. Like a guard at the frontier we wait in the darkness of prayer, ready to call out, 'Who goes there?' and the answer will come, 'I am that I am. I am the Way, I am the Truth, I am the Life. I am the Song – sing me! I am the Tune – play me!' Throughout the long hours of darkness each one of us is a Guardian of the Threshold.

In *The Hero with a Thousand Faces*, Joseph Campbell speaks of the psychological, spiritual and mythical implications of the journey to the Threshold. 'The adventure is always and everywhere a passage beyond the veil of the known into the unknown; the powers that watch at the boundary are dangerous; to deal with them is risky; yet for anyone with competence and courage the danger fades.'

Of course there is another meaning to the words 'to be in the way', and that is when we become an obstacle in our own path, when we block our own light, and become a stumbling block to ourselves as well as others. One of the things that we learn at the Threshold is how to step out of the way, how to let God empty us by filling us. It is only by stepping out of the way that we can be in the Way.

And on the Way there is not one threshold but many. Yet, if we remain at our post on the threshold of prayer we shall cross without fear the many other thresholds that await us.

Day 17

Encountering

It does not really matter what we do in our hour or half-hour of prayer. We do not even have to be consciously praying. St Anthony once remarked that the prayer of a monk is not perfect until he no longer realizes himself or the fact that he is praying. All we are asked to do is to be with Christ. In our everyday life, to spend an hour in the company of an intimate and deeply loved friend might mean the one talking and the other listening; it might mean lying in each other's arms, or making a meal together, or gardening. Whatever it is, we are content to be in one another's presence. Even a thousand miles apart lovers know what it is to rest in each other's presence. We become what we love. And so it should be in our relationship with Christ: let there be no strain. Human love also teaches us that those most dear to us are often closest in their absence. Thomas Merton has written how in solitude he came closest to an understanding and love of his own community.

In our hours with Christ we kneel or sit, quietly persevering in whatever form of prayer we have been led to practise. But there may be days when, perhaps deliberately, we just sit, open-eyed, aware of our surroundings, hearing the sound of the birds or the traffic, conscious of the life around us of which we are a part, and allowing ourselves to rest in these physical manifestations. Let us learn to hear God in the wind, to see Him in the light shafting through windows, be aware of Him in our fellows, even in those – especially those – who irritate us or whom we find it difficult to love. Or we may take up a book or a poem and read reflectively, even allowing ourselves to fall asleep. For in sleep God often speaks to us, as He does in dreams. If we fall asleep involuntarily we should not waste time in guilty feelings when we awake. More often than not we will find ourselves refreshed. It may be indolence, of course, that causes us to nod off, or it may be self-indulgence, but equally it may also be needful. We have to learn how to recognize the need for gentleness, for a holiday spirit. In particular the elderly should not worry, they who move in and out of sleep as naturally as a baby. We have to be gentle as well as tough with Sister or Brother Body. In this living and loving relationship with God we proceed by trial and error. Each hour of prayer is a fresh encounter with the Divine Lover and Beloved.

We learn about people by listening to them. We have to be patient. Above all we have to be patient with ourselves. We are so eager to be there in his arms, to be consumed with love – yet we do not really know what it is we are asking for, not knowing that our God is 'a consuming fire'. In his great mercy he protects us from the full blaze of his love. Let us rather, like the Woman of Samaria in Karol Wojtyla's poem, be grateful for the crumbs, for we can never, in this life, take all of him into ourselves:

> From this depth – I came only to draw water
> In a jug – so long ago, this brightness
> still clings to my eyes – the perception I found,
> and so much empty space, my own,
> reflected in the well.
> Yet it is good. I can never take all of you
> into me. Stay then as a mirror in the well.

We must persevere in season and out, accepting the fact that some days are full of distractions, squalls and winds and biting frosts, while others are mild and warm and cloudless. The weather changes, and instead of resenting this we learn to rejoice in the many moods. This weather shapes our interior landscape just as the weather in nature shapes the hills, trees and rocks.

Day 18

Looking

Meditation sharpens the sight and the insight. We begin to perceive that every moment is capable of Epiphany. 'Look at the birds of the air!' says Jesus, and we have but to look at one bird, the jay, to perceive the Logos at work in creation. The jay has a specialized knowledge of how best to plant oak and beech trees that still amazes the experienced forester. Left to themselves, these trees cannot successfully reproduce themselves, for acorns and beechnuts would merely lie at the base where they had fallen, unable to grow well in the shade of their species. Therefore the forester has to operate artificially. The jay, however, fills its crop with acorns and beechnuts and sticks them into the soil far more skilfully than any forester. It never puts several acorns together but always at correct planting distances, often in rows. Nature repeatedly reveals to us a deeper pattern, evidence of the Eternal Mind at work. We have to look up, to use our eyes and ears and, as Wordsworth reminds us,

> Hence in a season of calm weather
> though inland far we be,
> Our souls have sight of that immortal sea
> which brought us hither.

Or, as Francis Thompson expressed it,

> Turn but a stone and start a wing!
> 'Tis ye, 'tis your estranged faces
> That miss the many splendoured thing.

The greater reality is constantly breaking through in the most unexpected ways: through a widow's pension, a small boy's picnic meal, or friends breaking bread off the Emmaus Road. Epiphanies are everywhere. The majesty of the night sky with its myriad of stars seen in the heart of Africa or on a hilltop in Wales speaks of the majesty of the universe. Yet the image of the sky as a blanket with holes through which the light on the other side is breaking through is still valid as an image of a greater truth. Epiphany is the breaking through of the light, and, as William Blake teaches us, it is through the cracks that the light breaks through. Cracks also disfigure the smooth surface of our lives as surely as they do a ceiling or a wall; cracks are those things that disturb, pain, anger and bewilder us. Through the painful experiences light can break through into a new epiphany. The Eucharist itself is such a crack – not a reappearance but the revelation of something existing in eternity. Epiphany can come upon us anywhere.

I knew it once in a tiny churchyard in Herefordshire. There had been deep snow, but it had all gone when I drove over to take the early Eucharist for the tiny congregation. Walking in the churchyard before the service I noticed one last patch of snow in a corner. As I approached I saw that it was a clump of snowdrops that had pushed their way up through the snow. And I thought back to the time I was in Helsinki, when the snows began to thaw and revealed underneath the battered, crushed and yellow grass and how I thought then: I am like that grass, yet like that grass I too will revive and spring up afresh, green and sturdy.

That memory and that clump of snowdrops took me back to those words of George Herbert's which I read daily from the Divine Office for many weeks following my mother's death.

> Who would have thought my shrivelled heart
> Could have recovered greeness? It was gone
> Quite underground as flowers depart
> To feed their mother-root when they have blown;
> Where they together
> All the hard weather
> Dead to the world, keep house unknown.

And so that morning, by that ancient church, I stooped and picked a few snowdrops and took them in to the service where I gave them to Becky, a small girl who has difficulty in speaking but who has learned to say 'Amen!' and shouts it out joyfully at intervals; and often I call back to her, 'Amen, Becky!' On that morning those few snowdrops were as much a moment of epiphany for Becky as they were for me. The world indeed is charged with the grandeur of God. In meditation our eyes are opened and we see trees walking.

Day 19

Changing

Each of us has a story to tell, one life to live, one song to sing. The deep fear of most people is less that of physical death than of dying with their story untold, their life unlived, their song unsung. Every human being, says Jung, has a unique story, and no man can discover his greatest meaning unless he lives and, as it were, grows his own story. Should he lose it, or fail to live it, he loses his meaning and dies. As Laurens van der Post observes, 'One must be ready to obey the story and add one's mite to it. . . . I might even say in hindsight that obedience to the private and most intimate summons of the imagination is to live symbolically and religiously.'

NB → To obey one's story, to heed the inner images that well up, is a painful process, yet, to quote Robert Frost once again, 'We live by shedding.' The agony of breaking through personal limitations and going beyond them is the agony of spiritual growth; it is a process that all creative artists know. Art, literature and myth are instruments to help us past our limited and limiting horizons as we cross threshold after threshold. In the Sumerian *Epic of Gilgamesh* the hero searches for the answer to the meaning of life and death. At each frontier he is questioned afresh, 'Why are your cheeks so starved and your face so drawn? Why is despair in your heart and your face like the face of one who has made a long journey? For what reason have you made this great journey, crossing the seas whose passage is difficult? Tell me the reason for your coming?' And each time Gilgamesh answers, 'It is to see Utnapishtim whom we call the Faraway that I have come this journey. For this have I wandered over the world, I have crossed

many difficult ranges, I have crossed the seas, I have wearied
myself with travelling; my joints are aching, and I have lost
acquaintance with sleep. . . . O Father Utnapishtim, you who
have entered the assembly of the gods, I wish to question you
concerning the living and the dead, how shall I find the life for
which I am searching?'

Spiritual growth means the growth of the whole psyche. No
amount of praying will enable us to grow spiritually unless our
whole life is opened up to the influence of the Spirit. Those who
are locked into their own opinions, self-importance or prejudice;
those who are afraid to change, to give up, to let go; those who do
not even begin to listen to others, who cannot entertain contrasting viewpoints or alternative lifestyles; those who persistently
ignore the counsel of their dreams or of their bodies (for the body,
too, has its own wisdom); all these are refusing to grow
spiritually.

No amount of cutting weeds on a lawn will prevent the weeds
spreading. Until the roots are dealt with the weeds will merely
multiply. For several summers in Wales I observed countless
small shoots all over the lawn which, however often they were
mown, appeared to grow stronger. Finally I dug down and
discovered that all across the lawn, like varicose veins, extended a
network of tough, woody shoots, so that the lawn had to have
incisions made all over it before the long sinewy, snakelike roots
could be ripped out. It takes courage to carry out such surgery,
whether on a lawn or on one's self. Most people prefer to cling to
their neuroses, their illnesses, their prejudices, their established
patterns of work and behaviour, their familiar social and
domestic routines. Any suggestion of change threatens them, for
change means upheaval, and once you start more change will
follow. Change is an uncomfortable business – it leads to
unknown and unexpected adventures, it means letting go of our
psychological and emotional possessions.

To be open to change is to be willing to go on journeys of the
spirit. At the end of *King Lear* Kent is able to say, 'I have a journey
yet to go', and in *The Four Quartets* T. S. Eliot reminds us, 'Old
men should be explorers', while Emily Dickinson, the recluse of
Amherst who never saw the sea, still understood about the nature
of true voyaging when she wrote,

> Exultation is the going
> Of an inland soul to sea;
> Past the houses, past the headlands,
> Into deep eternity.

True spiritual growth means a willingness to travel. There can be no standing still. In *To Be a Pilgrim* Joyce Cary wrote, 'We must renew ourselves or die. We must make new worlds about us for the old does not last. Those who cling to this world must be dragged backwards into the womb which is also the grave. We are the pilgrims who must sleep every night beneath a new sky, for either we go forward to the new camp or the whirling earth carries us to the one behind. There is no choice but to move, forwards or backwards.'

Day 20

Words

Gertrude Stein was not being pretentious when she wrote, 'A rose is a rose is a rose is a rose.' She was trying to emphasize the essence of the rose, to make us look beyond the label; to look at the rose as though for the first time, as a child might experience a rose before it knows what it is called. We live in an age when words not merely swamp and engulf us but are misused, distorted, perverted and debunked. We use words like 'peace', 'God', 'love', 'salvation', and we do not take time to reflect, to experience what we mean by 'peace', 'God', 'love', 'salvation'. 'Words, words, words!' as Hamlet says. It is no wonder that theologians found it necessary to propose the concept: God is dead. It is not that the eternal reality of God has ceased to be, but that the word 'God' has become for many a stumbling block, preventing the experience of God.

At its most superficial a word conveys information and, as such, words act as signs: 'exit', 'saloon', 'drugstore', 'danger'; but words are also symbols pointing the way to the word as *logos* or meaning: 'In the beginning was meaning' is another translation of St John's opening words. 'Tree', 'bird', 'bread', 'wine', 'fire', 'water', 'garden' and many such words are still potent symbols, as people's dreams continue to reveal. Those who have argued for changing the imagery of the Bible, maintaining that references to shepherds and so forth are no longer relevant in a technological society, entirely miss the point that many such words are archetypal in content. Again, as so often, Emily Dickinson sets the matter in perspective – 'checks' is her word for chart:

> I never saw a Moor –
> I never saw the Sea –
> Yet know I how the Heather looks
> And what a billow be.
>
> I never spoke with God
> Nor visited in Heaven –
> Yet certain am I of the spot
> As if the Checks were given.

Human hearts have held all such images for thousands of years. Their silence invades us. Although they are words, yet we experience them wordlessly. They have power to move us deeply. Paradoxically we use words to express that which we cannot put into words:

> Silence is the perfect'st herald of joy;
> I were little happy if I could say how much.

Karol Wojtyla remarks in a poem,

> Sometimes it happens in conversation: we stand
> facing truth, and lack the words,
> have no gesture, no sign,
> And yet, we feel, no words, no gesture
> Or sign would convey the whole image
> that we must enter alone and face like Jacob.

It is here that prayer comes in. As we meditate upon certain texts or words, using them as mantras, the underlying mystery and silence behind and within these words slowly well up and begin to penetrate us with their life and joy, their peace and energy. 'Words,' said Robert Frost, 'exist in the mouth, not in books. You can't fix them and you don't want to fix them. You want them to adapt their sound to persons and places and times. You want them to change and be different.' He also once remarked to me how in his life there had been certain words, certain lines of great poems, that had haunted him, acting like lodestones – lines such as 'He that has power to hurt and will do none'; that, he said, had meant much to him. And on my own journey many lines of poetry or prose have acted as signposts pointing me onwards and inwards. The repetition also of the Divine Office, year in, year out, immerses one in the long tradition of man and woman's journey into God. Certain lines, appearing with regularity, have a way of rising to the surface of one's consciousness, speaking to one's condition; lines such as:

> As one whom his mother comforts

> My heart is ready, O my God

> Their life is like a watered garden

The artist John Rowlands Pritchard takes words and creates calligraphic icons. Many of his works hang on my walls so that, as I move about the house, they have a way of quietly seeping into me. Words painted on a wall or on an arch can act as powerful images, and I shall always remember a Carmelite monastery I used often to visit in London and the words painted over an arch in the cloister: 'In Carmel and at the Judgement I am alone with God.'

In the theatre the text of a play conveys information, but the real heart of the situation is often hidden in the sub-text, to which it is the task of actors and their director to find their way. The text itself may be very simple, perhaps the words 'I love you.' The text is like an iceberg, and the actor and director must discover what lies beneath the surface. In any one scene, at any one moment, a character may be *saying* one thing, *doing* something else, *thinking* yet another thought and *feeling* something quite different. In real life we often carry several thoughts and feelings simultaneously. I may be *saying*, 'I love you', in what I imagine to be ardent tones, but I may be looking elsewhere than at my beloved, and I may be thinking or feeling:

1. Well, I do love you *but* . . .
2. Not at this particular moment . . .
3. At least, I wish I could get this pipe to light . . .
4. I wonder if she's going to ask what I was doing yesterday afternoon when she rang and I wasn't in my office . . .
5. She's looking older tonight – she's getting quite a double chin . . .
6. Must watch my weight, oughtn't to drink so much beer . . .
7. Now why am I saying 'I love you' at this moment?

A whole soliloquy of such thoughts races through our minds at any one second, and my main motive at such a moment may perhaps be something as simple as 'I'm hungry. I wish we could eat', or it may be that behind thought No.4 lies a more complex motive of guilt.

Sometimes it is a single word that sets a challenge to the actor, such as the closing line of Ibsen's *Ghosts*: 'The sun, the sun, the sun, the sun, the sun!' It is how these words are said, the life within them, that creates theatre. If we stop short at the surface meaning of words we shall never experience them as living words, but if we meditate upon them they will become engraved upon the inner being. They will become the words of secret silence of which John Rowlands Pritchard speaks. In the beginning was the Word.

Day 21

The Lonely Place

'And Jacob was left alone and a man wrestled with him until the breaking of the day.' Because Jacob will not yield to the man – who is an angel in disguise – he has to be wounded. Only then does he ask the stranger for a blessing. It is at that moment that Jacob, as in an initiation ceremony, receives a new name – Israel.

Of Jesus we read that he frequently went apart into a lonely place and prayed. Loneliness is at the heart of prayer. I think it is the Venerable Chogyam Trungpa who says that meditation should be boring – as boring as possible – because only in intense boredom are all our habitual responses and concepts dissolved. The mind has a terror of boredom and loneliness, for it suspects that by means of such an intense experience another level of reality may be reached that will threaten its pretensions.

Rather than face monotony, boredom and loneliness we – especially in the West – fill up every conceivable hour with activity to prop up our fragile sense of identity and imagined usefulness. Social, domestic, professional, trivial and sensual activities crowd out the possibility of any empty spaces within us, or of an encounter with the dark angel who has come to wound us so that we may be healed. We are impatient for movement and do not know how to contain our restlessness within a nave of silence. It is a very common hazard among the caring professions, from doctors and priests to counsellors, healers and therapists, who are often so busy with other people's problems that often, quite unknowingly, they have no time for their own problems and evade that ultimate appointment with their own selves.

But loneliness, like boredom, is, as Emily Dickinson knew, the maker of souls.

> The Loneliness One dare not sound
> And would as soon surmise
> As in its Grave go plumbing
> To ascertain the size –
>
> The Loneliness whose worst alarm
> Is lest itself should see –
> And perish from before itself
> For just a scrutiny –
>
> The Horror not to be surveyed,
> But skirted in the Dark –
> With Consciousness suspended –
> And Being under lock
>
> I fear me this – is Loneliness –
> The Maker of the soul
> Its caverns and its corridors
> Illuminate or seal.

In loneliness we have to confront 'ourself behind ourself concealed'. As failures, bitternesses, betrayals, woundings and our own obstinacies well up, so we have to deal with them, or else repress and suppress them, in which case they will only renew their attacks. However, in the prayer of meditation, though they may arise as distractions, that is not the time for confronting them. Something else, however, happens. In our meditation, holding firmly to the centre, even while assailed by our many selves, we rest in the darkness, the emptiness and the aloneness that is God, and slowly, over the hours, months and years, something mysterious begins to happen. Gently, barely discernible, our souls and our psyches are purified. The silence of meditation, provided we truly surrender ourselves to the divine darkness, loosens psychological knots, dissolves subconscious coagulations, and drains away those secret poisons that invade our psyches.

Loneliness is central to the human condition; it is the secret plague that, for all our technological and material progress, invades and attacks Western society more insidiously than any germ warfare. No husband, wife, lover, or work can ultimately satisfy the depths of loneliness in each of us. No lover can satisfy such hunger. Those resounding words of St Augustine's still echo across the centuries, 'Thou, O Lord, hast made us for Thyself, and our hearts are restless until they find their rest in Thee. . . . Late have I loved Thee, O beauty both ancient and new, late have I loved Thee. You called, You cried out, and you rid me of my deafness.'

All those who go from partner to partner, skipping from bed to bed, divorce to divorce, job to job, distraction to distraction, are in search of a mirage. We may create beautiful homes, gardens, families, circles of friends, but all too often we are creating a mirror that reflects merely our own image. Behind all our busyness a superior spectre awaits us,

> One need not be a Chamber to be Haunted –
> One need not be a House –
> The Brain has Corridors – surpassing
> Material place –
>
> Far safer, of a Midnight Meeting
> External Ghost
> Than its interior confronting
> That cooler Host.
>
> Far safer, through an Abbey gallop,
> The Stones a 'chase –
> Than Unarmed, one's self encounter –
> In Lonesome Place –
>
> Ourself behind ourself, concealed –
> Should startle most –
> Assassin hid in our Apartment
> Be Horror's least.
>
> The Body – borrows a revolver –
> He bolts the Door –
> O'erlooking a superior spectre –
> Or More.

Emily Dickinson

We must therefore go apart into a lonely place to keep our appointment. Above all, those who are called to be priests, religious, counsellors or healers have an even greater need to go apart – 'For their sakes I sanctify myself.' In *A Journey in Ladakh* the young Rinpoche points the way for all of us when he says,

'Everyone of our generation lives in a fragmented, complex, disturbing time, in which it is hard to keep one's spiritual balance, hard to find the time to build that balance in the first place. I feel increasingly that I must go into retreat more, must meditate more, must discipline myself more. Otherwise I shall be of no use to my people.'

The clergy especially have a need to nurture their inner life. Perhaps the frenetic activity of so many clergy, especially in America, (at the other end of the scale is the apathy of defeatism) stems from the general crisis of identity among most clergy, Roman and Anglican. In *The Wounded Healer* Father Henri Nouwen writes, 'The wound of loneliness in the life of the minister hurts all the more since he finds that his professional impact on others is diminishing.'

The priest is the guardian of an order that is greater than personal vision and, as I have indicated in the opening section of this book, it may well be that today it is the contemplative side of his vocation that is the most important to nurture. Paradoxically, those who learn how to be alone with their aloneness will draw others to them. The desert fathers, the holy men of India in their caves and ashrams, Mother Julian in her cell in Norwich, Père de Foucauld in the desert, Abhishiktananda in his cave in India, the Little Brothers and Sisters of Jesus in their cells in city and country, all hermits and anchorites everywhere, speak to our society in a way that is urgently needed. Solitary in their caves, alone with the Alone, they draw us gently, inescapably, to the love and compassion of God, as surely as migrating birds return to their place of origin. If we use the other meaning of the word 'Abba' we can pray thus, 'Our place of origin, which is in Heaven. . . .'

Day 22

Frontier

In *The Epic of Gilgamesh* we read how Gilgamesh sets out on a great journey to discover the secret of everlasting life. When he reaches the first frontier of the mountains he is challenged by one of the guardians. 'Why have you come so great a journey? For what have you travelled so far, crossing the dangerous waters? Tell me the reason for your coming.' The answers to such questions are always to be found at the frontier or on the other side of the frontier.

There are many kinds of frontier. There are those between one generation and another, one race and another, north and south, black people and white, Dr Jekyll and Mr Hyde, good and evil. These frontiers may be visualized as a gap, a ravine, a fence, Offa's Dyke, a fence, an Iron Curtain, even a simple wall as in Robert Frost's poem 'Mending Wall.' Frost describes how in spring he and his neighbour walk the pastures to mend the stone wall between their properties.

> Before I built a wall I'd ask to know
> What I was walling in or walling out,
> And to whom I was like to give offence.
> Something there is that doesn't like a wall,
> That wants it down.

A frontier marks the division between one territory and another. A journey to a frontier is often one from the known to the unknown. What lies on the other side may be desired – an El Dorado of our dreams, a Utopia, or it may be Hades, the Burning Fiery Furnace, the Waste Land. Mythology and the history of religions are full of stories and rituals relating to the departure of a dead man's soul from the world and its journey to the distant land of spirits. Many tales are told of journeys across the River Styx to Hades: the descent of Orpheus to bring back Eurydice, of Dionysus to bring back Semele, and the voyage of Odysseus to the ends of the ocean. The daily descent of the sun beneath the frontier of the horizon led naturally to a belief that a Land of Departed Souls lay in the Far West, in the World Below. And if mortals could cross this frontier to the world beyond it was equally possible for spirits to cross over from the other side. Small children cross backwards and forwards with ease over these frontiers of the imagination: a child looking at itself in the mirror has an intimation of such possibilities.

The history of Shamanism is full of accounts of similar journeys by shamans in trance. 'To reach the Land of the Dead,' writes Andreas Lommel in *The World of the Early Hunters*, 'the Greenland shaman has to go down to the bottom of the sea, whose realm (mythologically conceived) is separated from the Land of the Dead by a river – the frontier between the Land of the Dead and the World of the Living.'

Tennessee Williams's play *Camino Real* concerns the attempt by various characters to cross or not cross the frontier. The Land Beyond the Mountains, we are told, is known as Terra Incognita (the unknown land). Don Quixote tells us that he wears a bit of faded blue ribbon to remind himself, as an old knight, of the distance that he has gone and the distance he has yet to go. Later in the play Marguérite, La Dame aux Camélias, says to her lover, Casanova, 'You don't really want to leave here. The truth of the matter is that you're terrified of the Terra Incognita outside that wall!' to which he replies, 'You've hit upon the truth. I am terrified of the unknown country inside or outside this wall or any place on earth without you with me.'

Lord Byron, the artist, successfully escapes. 'It is time to leave here,' he announces. 'There is a time for departure even when there's no certain place to go. *Make voyages*! *Attempt them*! There is nothing else.' However, when Marguérite attempts to leave on the plane called the Fugitivo, she discovers that there is no reservation in her name and that her papers are lost; she has no passport, no identity, no means of moving on. Like Blanche du

Bois in *A Streetcar Named Desire*, she has reached the point of no
return. Tennessee Williams's play is a moving allegory of today.
So many people, especially the young, are metaphorically
without passports, without identity. They do not know who they
are, where they have come from – America, and Western society
in general, is increasingly a rootless society – nor where they are
going. Of course when we are young we do not always know, or
even sense, our ultimate destination, but we must be driven by an
inner impetus if we are to cross our own frontier and discover our
own potential. The deep sadness of today's society is that so many
of its members are inhibited by the fear of atomic annihilation
and a feeling of having no control over their destiny.

One of the exercises which I use in my ritual workshops
involves crossing a frontier. The results are always uniquely
different for each individual, revealing much about the inner
journey of that person. For each who undertakes the exercise the
frontier will have its own associations. Some seek to return from
it; some find that, having got there, they cannot, and that once
they have crossed it there is no point of return. Others journey
with great difficulty and apprehension, only to find that once they
have crossed over there is a release of energy and a feeling of new
growth. They are the ones who have 'sight of that eternal sea that
brought us hither' and so they journey on. Some, like Emily
Dickinson, realize that the frontier can be deceptive,

> A loss of something ever felt I . . .
> And a suspicion like a finger
> Touches my forehead now and then
> That I am looking oppositely
> For the site of the Kingdom of Heaven.

All myths, all personal responses concerning the frontier are, of
course, maps of an interior reality. At the deepest level the
frontier is within each one of us. As an inner reality the frontier
has to be crossed again and again as, like Gilgamesh, we search
for the continuously unfolding mystery of life and its meaning.
Only at the end of the journey may it be said of us, hopefully, as it
was said of Gilgamesh, 'He was wise, he saw mysteries, and knew
secret things. He went a long journey, was weary, worn out with
labour, and returning, engraved on a stone the whole story.'

It is not surprising that the frontier as an image should appear with regularity in people's dreams. Dreams themselves are a frontier between the world of the conscious and the unconscious. Dreams bring us messages from the hinterland. Throughout the Bible, throughout literature and still today the dream continues to manifest itself. In St Matthews's Gospel we read, 'When Joseph awoke from his sleep he did as the angel commanded him.' In Shakespeare's *Pericles*, after the King is healed he hears the music of the spheres and falls at once into a profound sleep in which the goddess Diana appears to him in a dream. She commands Pericles to go to her temple and make offerings, and concludes with these words, 'Awake and tell thy dream.'

Many dreams are superficial, a tangle of the previous day's experiences exacerbated by indigestion. But the important dreams always declare themselves, provided we are alert; indeed, on occasion they thrust themselves upon our attention with all the intensity of a nightmare. When we awake from such a dream, even if it is in the middle of the night we should at once write it down. Later we need to reflect on it in the same way that we stand in front of a work of art, not examining it cerebrally but surrendering to its images, allowing them to work on us. In silence, in meditation, we must ponder these messages from beyond the frontier. When we have absorbed them we must act upon their instructions, remembering the words of God to Moses 'See that you work to the design which I showed you on the mountain.'

Day 23

Talking to God

Every six months or so I go to have my ears syringed by a naturopath doctor who uses an old Red Indian technique which involves placing a long wax tube into the ear. The other end is lit and, as it slowly burns, the heat melts the wax inside the ear and draws it up into the tube. For anyone who, like myself, has tinnitus, this is a much gentler way of extracting wax than the more conventional method of water suction. But I also enjoy going to see the gentle, humorous, inquiring American for his conversation. He is an Hasidic Jew and it was from him that I learned about a particular Hasidic form of prayer in which one is encouraged to stand alone, out of doors, and talk aloud to God about the smallest thing that concerns one. The intention is that one should turn to God, like a child to its parent, in absolute trust.

Prayer in every tradition is quite simply talking and listening to God. If we have never been able to talk to God it may help to try this approach, allowing thoughts and feelings – even feelings of anger and despair – to well up spontaneously. *Even* such feelings? Especially. Prayer has become too closely associated with piety, and has become genteel in consequence. It is important not to block off feelings, but rather to allow them expression. The Psalmist understood this. All our negative emotions are like wax: once it is removed we can hear God speaking.

There are many ways in which to approach God. At the highest level is canonical prayer, the prayer of the whole Church, using a liturgy that has evolved over the centuries, speaking on behalf of all women, men and children – all creation. This great prayer of the Church includes praise, thanksgiving and intercession. But

there is also the prayer of the individual, which can take two
forms: one is the deliberate emptying of the self in meditation so
that God may enter in; and there is this talking directly to God in
our own words, which, unlike meditation, does not try to hold
back thoughts and feelings but allows them full expression. Some
will respond to the first way, some to the other, and some will
move between the two. Sometimes people work too hard at
meditation (once again the ego getting in the way), and then they
need to release their spontaneity in this way. The results are often
very vivid, surprising and illuminating, especially if they are
written down.

It is also possible to draw or paint such a dialogue with God.
All we have to do is sit quietly at a table with pens, brushes or
pencils and blank paper, waiting quietly until the pen wants to
move. It really is a form of controlled doodling. The first few
efforts may be entirely meaningless. Slowly, however, with
practice, images will appear. We should not be afraid to draw
with the crudity and directness of a child, using stick figures if we
cannot draw real people. We are not aiming at creating for an art
class, but at allowing the images to well up. Once the drawing is
complete – and we will learn to sense when it is ended – we should
reflect on it. Sometimes such drawings can have all the humour,
practicality and forcefulness of a wise teacher speaking to us,
pointing almost dramatically to what is blocking us, or indicating
a direction in which we should go. More rarely such drawings can
have a visionary quality that goes beyond the personal. It is how
all creative artists work. The great artists are like deep sea divers
who on our behalf plunge into the depths of the unconscious and
return to the surface carrying images and icons of great power.
But the creative process itself is available to everyone and can be
used to enrich the life of the spirit. Among the Eskimo communities in Canada, and in certain other parts of the world, there
exist shamans.

A shaman is the artist-teacher-healer-priest of such a community. During his long period of novitiate he cries out at
intervals, 'All this because I wish to become seeing!' This is the
task of each one of us, and especially of the artist today. So many
have ears but cannot hear, have eyes but cannot see, have hearts

but do not respond. All art is concerned with things primal. It leads us back to our roots, to the space within. Its source is the silence at the centre of each one of us.

Day 24

Intercession

It is often after a period of silent meditation, or when we awake in the middle of the night, that we are most vulnerable; when the ego is lessened and the mind still that the Spirit can make itself felt. If we awake thinking of someone we should always heed that signal, and the stronger it is the more immediate should be our response. Such messages can sometimes come through with great urgency and should be responded to in the same spirit. Once I was woken by such a sense of someone calling to me, a friend who had been dying for months of a brain tumour. I got up and remained for an hour in prayer. She was vividly present and I knew that my task was simply to stay with her and hold her in the Divine Presence. There was a strong sensation of her preparing to cross over, and a great joy. A few hours later I was woken by the telephone and a friend saying, 'I thought you would want to know that Marion died in the small hours of this morning.'

As with dreams, such promptings must be heeded. It is very like learning how and when to speak at a Quaker meeting for worship. The first prompting to speak might well be the ego wanting to assert itself, and so one waits. If the thought persists then we must rise and speak, however nervous we are. In time one learns how to recognize the prompting of the Holy Spirit and to obey it without question. In the same way we may sometimes feel a prompting to get in touch with someone whom we have not seen for a long time. If the prompting is very strong and they are within reasonable distance we should go at once or, at the very least, telephone them. There are too many incidents of people having such intimations and then dismissing them as mere fancy, only to learn subsequently that the person in question was in real need of contact.

The practice of meditation will heighten our awareness of and response to such signals. We may not have spoken to someone for years; it may be that a misunderstanding has grown up, or there may be a real antagonism. It may have been our fault in the first instance, or the other person's, or both; but there comes a day when the prompting comes to go and see them, in an attempt to break the deadlock. However nervous we feel, we must heed it and risk being rebuffed. This raises the question: For whom do we pray? It is easy enough, as Jesus remarked, to pray for those we love, or those who ask us to pray for them: but it is equally important to pray for those we do not like, those whom we find it difficult to love, those who have wounded us or who are our enemies. We should never forget, moreover, that when two people fall out both are wounded. If someone maligns, libels or savages us and we are innocent – or even if we are not innocent – the attacker also is wounded. The extent to which our own wounds are healed under God will influence the healing of the other person's wounds.

We should constantly pray for those whom we would prefer to forget. We are all involved with one another and we cannot cut one another off with angry gestures and say, 'That's it, the friendship is over'. To do so is to create psychic and spiritual damage in the cosmos. Negative feelings and thoughts, anger and unresolved bitterness all pollute the atmosphere and poison our prayer. We cannot pray if there is rancour in our hearts and malice in our thoughts. I must.

We ought also to pray for the departed, and not just for a few days after their dying. As we get older the list becomes longer; nonetheless we should hold them in the presence of God, just as they also hold us. We pray for them, but they are also praying for us. The inter-relationship of the living and the departed is closer than we realize. If we truly believe in the communion of saints, there is nothing strange about this. In our dreams, and often on waking, we may have the experience of being visited by those who have already entered the realms of light. We are not alone.

What the dead had no speech for when living
They can tell you, being dead: the communication
Of the dead is tongued with fire, beyond the language of the living.
T. S. Eliot

Recent research has shown that many more people have such experiences than is generally realized, but they are usually unwilling to talk about them in case their family or neighbours think them peculiar. One such woman reported, 'Something woke me up. There was something or somebody by my bed. I wasn't frightened. Within ten minutes the torment that I'd felt, for some strange reason left me. I think I had more peace then than I'd had for a very long time. I have enough knowledge to know that there's Somebody there, to know that I need never be so alone again . . . he decided I needed help.' When asked who 'he' was, this woman replied, 'Jesus, I suppose.'

When such an experience comes it may last only a few seconds, but it is of such an intensity that it endures a lifetime, and is felt to be more real than observable reality. People often say they have no time for prayer, but apart from set times we have endless opportunities throughout the day when we can pray – whether we are walking to work, driving the car, queuing for a bus or travelling on the train. Many more people meditate nowadays and it is easy to recognize them on the train and subway. They sit with back erect, hands in lap, eyes closed; the Christian can learn much from their example. Each day, in fact, is crammed with opportunities when swift prayers can rise like fireworks in a night sky, exploding with love: fireworks of praise, thanksgiving and intercession.

Day 25

Angels

The practice of meditation will deepen our awareness of the many splendoured reality all about us. We will become increasingly aware that we are not alone – 'Turn but a stone and start a wing' – for the angels and spirits are all about us. A hundred years ago few people would have believed that men and women would fly about the world in aeroplanes and spaceships. Less than forty years ago who would have believed that men would walk on the moon? Such feats seemed no more than the imaginings of a Jules Verne or an H. G. Wells, yet the incredible has become credible within the space of one lifetime.

How strange, then, that our generation should find it difficult to believe in angels! For thousands of years people have believed in the existence of winged messengers who commute between time and eternity. For centuries the Christian Church believed in them, as did other religious cultures. Their appearances are recorded in history and scripture, while their forms have been carved and painted in countless cathedrals, basilicas, churches and temples throughout the world. And still today, even to people who are non-believers, angels continue to manifest themselves in dreams as they did centuries ago. Yet rarely today within the Church do we hear much about angels. Did they suddenly go out with technology? Are they now taboo? Certainly it would seem as though they are suddenly not very fashionable. It apparently does not worry the angels, for they continue to manifest themselves. For myself, I do not say that I believe in angels any more than I say that I believe in electricity, in atoms, or in the stars of the night sky. I cannot tell how these things work. I cannot even see them at work – but I know that they are there. I recall asking a Harley Street specialist, a distinguished and conservative man, what he thought about acupuncture. To my surprise he answered, 'Oh, there's no doubt that it works. We just don't know *how*, that's all.' So, too, with angels. They *are* there, but we cannot explain them. They belong to another order of time and space, as in Edwin Muir's poem 'The Annunciation'.

> The angel and the girl are met.
> Earth was the only meeting place.
> For the embodied never yet
> Travelled beyond the shore of space.
> The eternal spirits in freedom go.
>
> See, they have come together, see,
> While the destroying minutes flow,
> Each reflects the other's face
> Till heaven in hers and earth in his
> Shine steady there. He's come to her
> From far beyond the farthest star,
> Feathered through time. Immediacy
> Of strangest strangeness is the bliss
> That from their limbs all movement takes;
> Yet the increasing rapture brings
> So great a wonder that it makes
> Each feather tremble on his wing.

My own experience convinces me, teaches me, reassures me that the universe is full of presences, winged messengers – whatever we choose to call them. The word 'angel' is only an image pointing to the reality behind; we could as easily use another word or, like C. S. Lewis, invent a new name for them, 'eldrils'. These intelligences intervene and act on our behalf. Children are often closer to this other world, as are the elderly, the very sick or those in moments of extreme danger, exaltedness, fatigue or the deep quiet of meditation. At such moments we hear and sense a presence. We *know* that we are not alone. The veil that divides this world from the next, where there are no distinctions between today, yesterday and tomorrow, is at times almost transparent.

If throughout history people have described angels as clothed in white, winged, or bright with light, these are but attempts by the imagination to convey something of the speed, intensity and luminosity with which such messages, insights and intuitions are born and borne to us. And if all this seems strange to us we have but to recall the words of St Paul, 'The hidden wisdom of our God that we teach in our Mysteries, the things that no eye has seen, no ear has heard, things beyond the mind of man, that the spirit hath revealed.'

Angels, archangels, cherubim and seraphim – the ancient teachings suggest that there are many ranks and many tasks for the angelic host – are not out there but, as Francis Thompson reminds us,

> Not where the wheeling systems darken,
> And our benumbed conceiving soars! –
> The drift of pinions, would we hearken,
> Beats at our clay-shuttered doors!

To some is appointed the task of looking after us: to each of us an unseen companion, assisting us on our journey through time to eternity: 'Behold, I send an angel before you, to guard you on the way, and to bring you to the place which I have prepared. Give heed to him and hearken to his voice.'

Day 26

All Saints

With the beginning of November winter approaches and the dark encroaches. Putting the clocks back serves to shorten the days. The long and lonely nights of winter, the expectation of cold, wet and mist, of empty trees, grey skies and dead vegetation all weigh upon us. Depression often sets in along with the early nights, and winter ailments commence. We turn inwards on ourselves in a hibernation of the spirit. For the elderly, especially, the winter can be a long and lonely tunnel. In ancient times people feared that the sun was dying and that darkness would fall on the face of the earth, so they lit bonfires, made sacrifices, danced and uttered prayers that the sun would not die.

But the sun has already begun to die at the height of summer when on Midsummer's Day, at the time of the Summer Solstice, it begins its downward journey. It is as though at the centre of that great ball and blaze of light there is a tiny seed of darkness which, from that moment onwards, begins to eat up the sun. Then, at the time of the deepest darkness, at the Winter Solstice, in the Octave of Christmas, a tiny seed of light begins to glow in the ball of darkness, and from that the sun begins to revive and 'grow round again'. Always, yearly, for early man this was the miracle when the year turned upon its axis.

This mighty movement from light to darkness and darkness to light is fundamental to all nature and supernature. It is the law of Tao, this eternal swing between the dark and the light, between male and female, the active and the passive, God and Man, intellect and intuition, the straight and the curved, the Yin and the Yang. It is the union of all opposites of which mystics speak –

though not in a fixed position but in an endless dance.

The symbol of the Tao is that of a circle (itself a symbol of the cosmos) and this circle is divided into two segments, one black, one white. In the centre of the black is a white dot; in the centre of the white a black dot. Within the darkness the seed of light glows and grows, just as within the light a seed of darkness grows. Sometimes the darkness grows to such an extent that it appears about to engulf the light, but always at that point the process changes. To understand the law of changes is to understand more profoundly what is happening both within and without ourselves. The Tao (the Way) teaches us how to correspond with destiny. It is a matter not of predestination but of learning how to work with nature and supernature (or God), to correspond with the eternal dance. The Tao teaches us, as does all nature, that there is a time for doing and a time for not doing; a time for sowing and initiative and a time for waiting; just as there is a time for dying and a time for living.

Winter is a time for dying. Therefore it is not surprising that in the eighth century in the West the Church created the feast of All Saints at the onset of winter, grafting it upon a more ancient, pagan ceremony. I use the word 'pagan' in its primary meaning of 'outside the town . . . in the country'. People who live in the country are closer to the wisdom of nature and the unfolding life of the seasons than are those who live in cities. And the ancient druidical feast on which the Church founded its feast of All Saints was that of Saman, Lord of Death. On the night of his feast it was believed that witches and ghosts were abroad and that wicked souls escaped from hell, hence the lighting of Hallowe'en bonfires as a protection in the darkness.

Darkness, which is half of the Tao, is something that our ancestors understood more vividly than we do. They went to bed with the setting of the sun and they rose with the dawn. Beeswax candles were costly. One can easily imagine any church or cathedral deep in shadow on a winter's morning, with only the flickering of two candles on the altar reflected in the gilt and brocade of the priest's vestments, and the Blessed Sacrament in its monstrance rising like the sun itself.

> Now it is the time of night
> When the graves all gaping wide,

Everyone lets forth his sprite
In the churchway paths to glide.

Darkness is frightening to a child and, if we are honest, to most people. It obliterates all known landmarks, removes all sense of identity – which is why, in prayer, we must go through such darkness from time to time. But on the other side of that darkness is the brilliance of eternity. The ancient feast of All Saints marks the edge of this darkness. It speaks to us of the massive power of evil, not only 'out there' but all about us and within us. We do well to pray that our souls be protected from evil. But on this feast the Church encapsulates the whole movement of nature, of Advent to Christmas, Lent to Easter, winter to spring. At the very edge of darkness, as we light our candles of prayer, we are reminded that we are not alone but are encompassed about on every side by a mighty gathering, as is expressed in the Divine Office for this Feast: 'What you have come to is Mount Sion, the City of the Living God, the heavenly Jerusalem, where the millions of living angels have gathered for the festival with the whole Church in which everyone is a firstborn son and a citizen of heaven.'

Day 27

Tree

In New York a group of business executives came together for a week's course of psychological training. During the week they were all asked to take part in a guided fantasy journey. They were invited to imagine that they were planting a tree; then that they were that seed, putting down roots, sending forth shoots, pushing its way up to the light, growing, forming leaves and fruit, enduring many kinds of weather, and finally growing old. At the end, when the lights were turned up, each was invited to speak about the experience and to describe what tree each had been. One man replied, 'I didn't know what kind of a tree I was so I decided to wait until I put forth leaves and then I would know what I was.'

Each one of us has to know what kind of tree we are. Parents often say they would love their son to become a doctor, a lawyer or an architect. And the son becomes a doctor, lawyer or architect, when perhaps he would much rather have been a carpenter or an actor; like the young waiter at Joe Allen's in London whose father wanted him to go to Sandhurst, although the boy himself wanted to go to the Royal Academy of Dramatic Art to train as an actor. When his acceptance for both institutions arrived on the same day his father tore up the acceptance form from RADA and told him he was going to Sandhurst. After six months he left and decided to try again for RADA. He is one of the lucky ones, he has learned how to 'stop being theirs'. But many people will say at the end of their lives, 'I made a good living, but I never lived.' They will look back and say, 'I was such a good carpenter, but that wasn't acceptable to my family.'

To be a Christian means to be as truly one's self as Jesus was himself. The tragedy for so many people is that they reach the end of their lives and suddenly realize that they have been living someone else's life: their parent's, their lover's or society's. In the forest there are many trees. We have to find what tree we are and then we can take our place in the eternal orchard.

Day 28

Becoming

In any book about prayer it is all too easy to become lop-sided, as though one is saying, 'Meditate and all will be well.' However, we are creatures of body, emotions, intelligence and soul; the heart has its reasons and the body its own wisdom. If we neglect our bodies, do not feed them properly, exercise and rest them, they will become subject to illness. In meditation we should not shut out the body. If we are truly centred, then mind, body, soul and heart will be at rest like those great statues of the Buddha in the Caves of Polannaruwa in Ceylon which Thomas Merton describes so memorably in his last journal, *Asian Journey*.

Too much concentration upon the life of the spirit, especially in the beginner, can cause various kinds of mental and spiritual indigestion. We need to nourish our whole being. And just as it is said that we are what we eat, so similarly we are what we read and watch. We should read reflectively, allowing one book to lead us onto the next in an organic way; so too with music and art. The books we read, the sculptures and pictures we see, the music we hear, the jobs we choose to do, the people we encounter, all go to the making of our story, our own song. 'Select: select,' writes Edwin Muir; 'make an anthology of what's been given you by bold casual time. Revise: omit, keep what's significant.' As Malcolm Muggeridge once remarked, 'One's books accumulate round one like a coral reef – something one builds up out of one's life and activities.' We do not read, look or listen aimlessly, but selectively, allowing our selves to be shaped. Each person has different experiences and encounters. Each is on a different journey.

Some people, as part of their search for wholeness, will explore the Alexander Technique, Shiatsu, Tai Chi or various forms of analysis and therapy. Some have a strong need to move and dance; others to paint and sculpt. Some find that gardening, cooking, preparing a table for a special celebration or other forms of work, are creative ways of uniting body, mind, heart and spirit. All tasks can be grudging chores or they can be illuminated by the creativity within each of us, redeemed by love, healing and wholing in their effect. The more we allow ourselves to be in touch with our own centre the less hurried we become and the more open to each moment, aware of its uniqueness. If our daily work, especially repetitive tasks, is alien to our growth as men and women of the Spirit, we will receive clear instructions to change. I think of one of the most contented men I know. For many years he had been a stage designer and then one day, sitting on a hilltop, he said to himself, 'What do I really want to do with my life? Do I want merely to go on designing sets for the rest of my days?' And out of the sky came the word 'Earth', and the feeling that he wanted to work with the soil. He bought a bicycle and now has twenty gardens that he looks after, doing basic jobs only. He earns less than he might elsewhere but he is happy, and regularly attends a small church made famous by George Herbert.

Nothing is an end in itself, only a means to the one true end in which our lives are made meaningful, and we are in union with all sentient beings. The more we allow this process to unfold, the more it will flow into our praying and out again into our relationships with those around us, expressing itself in many different forms of social commitment. The inner life, the journey of the spirit, the life of prayer, is not self-enclosed like a garden created only for one's own delight. Once we have found the way to the centre our lives will become an open garden.

We have to work at ourselves, at our loves, at our relationships, at our work. Any neglect at any level results in an imbalance and can lead to psychosomatic illness or even psychic disorder. In our society today, even in the 'alternative' world, we pay lip service to certain ideals and concepts. We use words as glibly as any television commentator. A session in a Carl Rogers encounter group, however, would unmask most of us, especially the clergy –

which is perhaps why so few attend such sessions. Too many
Christians are acting a rôle, while their real authentic selves are
either not present or, worse, not even known.

In one of her last letters before entering Gurdjieff's* Institute at
Fontainebleau, the writer Katherine Mansfield wrote, 'I want to
be what I am becoming.' Conversion (*metanoia*) is a continuing
process and not of one moment only. In meditation the secret
activity is unfolding deep within. The Rev. Dr. Martin Israel has
written, 'As we grow into spiritual awareness so there is a greater
exposure of the depths within us . . . the Spirit unlocks the
person's inner life, opens him to the love and the wounding of his
brothers. . . . Faith is a state of being open to life's potentialities.
One gives one's self unreservedly to the moment.'

In prayer we become. We become more, not less, vulnerable.
That process of becoming is an eternal one, for as St Anselm
wrote in the *Proslogion*,

> O supreme and inaccessible Light! O whole and blessed truth! You
> are wholly present everywhere and I do not see you. In you I move
> and in you I have my being, and I cannot come near you. You are
> within me and around me, and I do not experience you with my
> senses.
>
> I pray, O God, that I know you and love you, so that I may rejoice
> in you. And if I cannot do so fully in this life, may I progress every
> day until all comes to fullness; let the knowledge of you grow in me
> here in this life, and there in heaven let it be complete; let your love
> grow in me here and reach fullness there, so that here my joy may be
> great in hope, and there be complete in reality.
>
> Until then, let my mind meditate on you, let my tongue speak of
> you, let my heart love you, let my mouth preach you. Let my soul
> hunger for you, let my flesh thirst for you, my whole being desire
> you, until I enter the joy of the Lord, who is God, Three in One,
> blessed for ever.

*Russian-born esoteric teacher (1877–1949)

Day 29

Seeing

We say the sky is blue, but what do we mean by that? The sky is not blue. It may be green, grey, mauve, crimson, black, white or blue, according to the time, season, or even our own mood. How do we see the blue of the sky before we say 'The sky is blue'? The English novelist Joyce Cary, described one of his children as a baby of fourteen months sitting in its pram watching a newspaper on the grass close by. There was a breeze along the ground and the newspaper was moving. Sometimes the top page swelled up and fluttered; sometimes two or three pages were moved and seemed to struggle together; sometimes the whole paper rose up on one side and flapped awkwardly for a few feet before tumbling down again. The child did not know that this object was a newspaper moved by the wind. It was watching with intense, absorbed curiosity a creature entirely new to its experience; and through the child's eyes Joyce Cary had a pure intuition of the newspaper as an object, as an individual thing at a specific moment.

Of course, a great deal of the spiritual joy that children bring us is just this of seeing the world as a new thing and so renewing for us the freshness of life. But they always lose this power of original expression as soon as they begin their education. In *Art and Reality* Cary has a description of a small child of seven who once asked him if he would like a drawing, and offered to draw a swan. The child sat down and drew for half an hour, and produced the most original swan the writer had ever seen. It was a swimming swan – that is, a creature designed simply to swim. Its feet were enormous and very carefully finished, obviously from life. The whole structure of the feet was shown in heavy black lines. The child was used to seeing swans on a canal at the end of her garden and had taken particular notice of their feet. Below the water the swan was all power. But for body she gave it the faintest, lightest outline, neck and wings included in one round line shaped rather like a cloud – a perfect expression of the cloudlike movement of the swan on the surface.

He was admiring this swan when an older child observed, 'That's not a swan! I'll draw you a swan,' and then produced a Christmas card type swan. 'Yet,' as Cary observed,

> the second child had all the qualities of the first, intelligence, sensiblity. A few years before, she had had the ability to see for herself, to receive the unique personal impression. She had lost it by the education which emphasises the fact, measurements, analysis, the concept. Education is, and must be, almost entirely conceptual. And the concept is always the enemy of the intuition. It is said that when you give a child the name of a bird, it loses the bird. It never *sees* the bird again, but only a sparrow, a thrush, a swan, and there is a good deal of truth in this. We all know people for whom all nature and art consists of concepts, whose life, therefore, is entirely bound up with objects known only under labels and never seen in their own quality.

How can we see the blue of the sky before we say, 'The sky is blue'? This is the theme of a poem by Wallace Stevens:

> Begin, ephebe, by perceiving the idea
> Of this invention, this invented world
> The inconceivable idea of the sun.
>
> You must become an ignorant man again
> And see the sun again with an ignorant eye
> And see it clearly in the idea of it . . .
>
> How clean the sun when seen in its idea,
> Washed in the remotest cleanliness of heaven
> That has expelled us and its images . . .
>
> The sun must bear no name – but be –
> In the difficulty of what it is to be.

And this, says Stevens, is one of the things that art is about,

> The poem refreshes life so that we share,
> For a moment, the first idea.

How can we see those about us before we affix the labels mother, father, lover, child, teacher, leader? Sadly, after a time so many husbands and wives, parents and children, teachers and students no longer look at or into each other. They see the label and not the person, and then they are surprised when the relationship breaks apart. Labels pin people down like butterflies in a frame; except, of course, that people cannot be compartmentalized like this. We fix the label and then cease to look, and so we do not see that the person is changing, growing or withering. In the same way people do not listen properly to one another; they are too busy making their own sound. I do not mean merely listening to the pattern of words being used, but to their rhythm, the *tone* of voice (which may be telling us something quite different from the message of the surface context of the words). We need to learn how to listen stethoscopically, as it were, in order to catch the hidden things, the things that are not said.

It is one thing to talk 'at' a person, as so many married couples do, but it is quite another thing to talk 'with' a person. A lover may say 'I love you', but the words are inadequate to convey the complexity of thoughts and feelings at that one moment of time. And how the words are said today will be very different from the way they are said tomorrow. A person may appear to be saying all the right things (think of any politician, and many a churchman also), and yet, intuitively, we know that these are hollow words.

We have to learn how to look long and deep and not be afraid: not be afraid of what we may find in ourselves or in the other person. How rarely people meet at such a level. When it happens, we recognize the truth of Shakespeare's line, 'Journeys end in lovers meeting.' The practice of wordless meditation, of prayer, leads to a deeper awareness of the sub-text in every meeting. We hear the words of secret silence.

Day 30

The Flame

I see an enormous towering statue of a Man, made of openwork gold, so that it appears light, insubstantial and floating, yet at the same time massive and strong. Approaching closer, I see that it is composed of thousands of minute bodies, intricately carved: the figures of men, women, children and babies; each one unique, with space between, yet linked to one another. At the base of this statue, by an ankle, I discover a door. I go through this and begin to climb a spiral staircase which leads to the centre so that now I am standing in the chest of this Man-God. Here I find a golden heart radiating light from a flame that burns perpetually inside it. Climbing higher still, I arrive at an upper chamber behind the eyes and I look out through the sockets, as though standing in a lighthouse. In this brain chamber are three figures on a wheel, spinning round, their hands linked in a circular dance. They are images of the Father and the Son and the Holy Spirit in their eternal dance. Then the whole statue dissolves, leaving only the light burning within the golden heart, like a tabernacle lamp. Then that, too, disappears and the flame is burning in my heart.

(from the author's journal)

Recently I came across these lines from the *Chandoga Upanishad*. 'In the Centre of the Castle of Brahma, our own body, there is a small shrine, in the form of a lotus flower and within can be found a small space. We should find who dwells there and want to know him, for the while universe is in him and he dwells within our heart.' We should indeed seek to know and understand that inhabitant. It is the fragment of the divine that is contained within each one of us. It is our task to nourish and kindle this light so that, like a lighthouse, its radiance spreads through all creation. As another Sufi poet, Ibu Arabi, put it, 'O ancient temple, there hath risen for you a light that gleams in our hearts.'

Images are necessary on the way. They will arise from the depths of the unconscious, unbidden, manifesting themselves for a time and then dissolving, their work completed. We must not hold onto them, nor grow dependent upon them. They arrive, we ponder them and let them go. All that should be left is the flame burning in the Eternal Presence. That is true prayer.

Day 31

The Fire

We must set aside all discursive operations of the intellect and turn the very apex of our soul to God to be entirely transformed in him. This is most mystical and secret. No one knows it but he who has received it. No one receives it but he who has desired it. No one desires it but he who is deeply penetrated by the fire of the Holy Spirit, the fire Christ sent on earth. This is why the apostle says that this mystical wisdom is revealed through the Holy Spirit.

If you want to understand how this happens, ask it of grace, not of learning; ask it of desire, not of understanding; ask it of earnest prayer, not of attentive reading; ask it of the betrothed, not of the teacher; ask it of God, not of man; ask it of darkness, not of radiance. Ask it not of light, but of fire that completely inflames you and transports you to God with extreme sweetness and burning affection. This fire is God himself.

From the Treatise of St. Bonaventure
The Journey of the Mind of God

After the Performance

"When the work of God is finished
Let all go out in deep silence"

THE HOLY RULE OF SAINT BENEDICT

Glossary of Terms

Atman Hindu term meaning the sub-stratum of consciousness, the self; apparently distinguishable from – but in reality identical with – the supreme being, Brahman.

Bodhisattva A being of Enlightenment, whose nature it is to strive for the salvation of all sentient beings through wisdom and compassion.

Brahman The supreme being of Hinduism, whose classical description is 'Neti, Neti' ('not this, not that').

Chela Pupil, disciple.

Chak ras In oriental philosophy, a series of energy points on the 'etheric' or spirit-body.

Guru Spiritual guide or preceptor.

Nirvana The Buddhist meaning is defined in Webster's *New International Dictionary* as 'The dying out in the heart of the threefold fire of *raga, dosa* and *moha*, or passion, hatred and delusion. This emancipation involves a beatific spiritual condition, and freedom from the necessity of future transmigration.'

Roshi A Zen master.

Samadhi Very deep, meditative concentration resulting in a state of mental calm and absence of distractions.

Samsara Process of birth and death; the round of existence where one phenomenon gives rise to another, like the successive waves of the sea.

Satori Zen Enlightenment, a Buddhist term for enlightened spirituality, an awakening.

Shiatsu In Japanese the word *shi* means finger and *atsu* pressure. Shiatsu, also called acupressure, is an Oriental massage in which the fingers are pressed on particular points of the body to ease aches, pains, tension, fatigue and symptoms of disease. There are 361 acupressure points and they are located along the 'meridian lines', the fourteen channels through which the body's energy flows. These channels are invisible, but according to Oriental philosophy exist as surely and indefinably as the nerves. Like acupuncture, when used skilfully Shiatsu can relieve many kinds of chronic problems and disabling aches and pains.

Shinto   A Japanese variant of Buddhism, often referred to as a nature religion.

Shaman   See **Shamanism**. The shaman is not merely a medicine man, a doctor or a man with priestly functions, but also a singer, dancer, painter and actor. He gives artistic shape to the inner images of the tribe or community and thereby brings about healing. (*See Shamanism: Techniques of Ecstasy* by Mircea Eliade, and *The World of the Early Hunters* by Andreas Lommel.)

Shamanism   Form of priestly lore originating with the peoples of Siberia and still a living force among some American Indians and Eskimos, and in certain areas of Japan and Tibet.

Sufi   Member of an Islamic religious order. The name derives from the white woollen robe worn by the initiated.

Sutra   The name given to the Buddhist scriptures.

Tai Chi   Meditation in movement, which energizes the body and calms the spirit. Tai Chi represents the ultimate unity, with its two faces of Yin (dark softness) and Yang (light toughness), Yin representing the feminine energy, and Yang the masculine. Tai Chi is represented by the well-known circle divided into two complementary teardrops, one light, the other dark. In the centre of the light teardrop is a point of dark Yin; in the centre of the dark one is a point of light Yang. Yang and Yin also represent, apart from male and female, good and bad, firm and yielding, day and night, north and south, heaven and earth, odd and even.

Tao Te Ching   Classic text of Taoism, traditionally believed to have been written by Lao Tzu (551–479 BC). Whether Lao Tzu is a historical figure or not, and if so whether he was the author or not, does not alter that fact that this and other Taoist writings have had an enduring impact on Chinese thought.

Upanishads   Inspired writings, originally in Sanskrit, which together with the *Vedas* and the *Bhagavad Gita* are the recognized sources of Hinduism.

Yang-Yin   The positive-negative polarization under which Chinese philosophers view the cosmos; e.g. male–female, light–darkness, fire–water. See also **Tai Chi**.

Acknowledgements

In the course of my own journey I have found help and inspiration in many writers, some of whom I have quoted from in the process of writing this book. The most important of these are:

Edwin Muir, *Collected Poems*, by permission of Faber and Faber;
Farid ud-Din Attar, *The Conference of the Birds*, translated by C. S. Nott, published by Routledge and Kegan Paul;
Victor Turner, *From Ritual to Theatre*, Performing Arts Journal, New York;
Virginia Woolf, *The Voyage Out*, Duckworth;
Emily Dickinson, *Complete Poems*, Faber and Faber;
Isamu Noguchi, *A Sculptor's World*, Thames and Hudson;
Iris Murdoch, *The Good Apprentice*, by permission of Chatto and Windus;
Abhishiktananda, *The Secret of Arunachala*, ISPCK, Delhi;
Brother Alban SSF, *Introduction to William of Glasshampton*, Geoffrey Curtis, SPCK;
Philip Toynbee, *Part of a Journey*, Collins;
Lao Tzu, *Tao te Ching*, trans. by D. C. Lau; Penguin Books, David Burrow's unpublished poem;
Peter Brook, *The Empty Space*, Penguin Books;
Gerard Manley Hopkins, *Selected Poems*, OUP;
C.P. Cavafy, *Collected Poems*, trans. by Rae Dalvern, by permission of Hogarth Press;
Robert Frost, *The Road not Taken*, *Poetry*, by permission of Jonathan Cape and the Estate of Robert Frost;
Andrew Harvey, *Journey in Ladakh*, by permission of Jonathan Cape and the Estate of Robert Frost;
Laurens van der Post, *Testament to the Bushmen* (with Jane Taylor), Viking Penguin;
Teilhard de Chardin, *Towards a New Mysticism* and *Le Milieu Divin*, Collins and Fontana respectively;

Anon, *The Ungainsayable Presence,* The Foundation Trust, The
Centaur Press;
Mircea Eliade, *Shamanism, Techniques of Archaic Ecstacy,* by permis-
sion of Routledge & Kegan Paul, *No Souvenirs, Journals 1957–69,* by
permission of Routledge and Kegan Paul, *Ordeal by Labyrinth:
Conversations with Mircea Eliade and Claude-Henri Rocquet,* trans. by
Derek Coltman, University of Chicago Press;
T. S. Eliot, *The Four Quartets,* by permission of Faber and Faber;
Joseph Gelineau, *The Shape of the Liturgy,* trans. by Dinah Livingstone,
Darton, Longman, Todd;
P. D. Mehta, *The Heart of Religion,* Compton Russell;
Thomas Merton, *Asian Journal,* by permission of Sheldon Press;
Dag Hammarskjold, *Markings,* Faber and Faber;
Shunrya Suzuki, *Zen Mind, Beginner's Mind,* Weatherhill;
K. G. von Durkheim, *Hara: The Vital Centre of Man,* Allen and Unwin;
Vincenzo Vannini, *Della Voce Umana;*translated by Joyce Warrack,
Alexander Journal;
Juan Mascaré (trans.), *Bhagavad Gita,* Penguin;
Dr Javad Nurbakhsh, *In the Tavern of Ruin,* Khanigahi-Nimatullahi
Publications, New York;
Elsie Mitchell, *Sun Buddhas, Moon Buddhas,* Weatherhill;
Chogyam Trungpa, *Meditation in Action,* Stuart and Watkins;
T. H. White, *The Goshawk,* Longman;
Idries Shah, *The Way of the Sufi,* Cape;
John Rowlands Pritchard, Unpublished poem;
Georges Bernanos, *Les Dialogues des Carmelites,* trans. by M. Legat;
Karol Wojtyla, *Easter Vigil and Other Poems,* trans. by J. Peterkiewicz,
Hutchinson, 1979;
The Journals of Brother Roger Schutz of Taizé, by permission of
Mowbrays;
Malcolm Muggeridge, *Something Beautiful for God,* by permission of
Collins;
P. M. Matarosso (trans), *The Quest of the Holy Grail,* Penguin;
Joseph Campbell, *The Hero with a Thousand Faces,* Abacus;
C. G. Jung, *Psychology and Alchemy,* Collected Works, Vol 12, by
permission of Routledge and Kegan Paul;
K. O. Schmidt, *The Message of the Grail,* CSA Press, Georgia;
N. K. Sanders (trans), *The Epic of Gilgamesh,* by permission of Penguin
Books;
Joyce Cary, *To be a Pilgrim,* Michael Joseph, and *Art and Reality*
(Collected Essays, Michael Joseph);
Martin Israel, *The Smouldering Fire,* Hodder and Stoughton;
Wallace Stevens, *Collected Poems,* by permission of Faber and Faber.